# Send in the Wolves

The Million Dollar, Real-World Education
On How To Run A Successful, Profitable
Business In This New Economy...

JIM TONER & JOHN MULRY

ISBN-13: 978-0-9928003-3-8

*Send in the Wolves* is available at special quantity discounts for bulk purchases, for sales promotions, premiums, fundraising, and educational use. For more information, please write to the below address.

Published by: Expect Success Academy, Unit 14, Ballybane, Enterprise Centre, Galway, Ireland

www.SendintheWolves.com

First Edition, 2017

Edited by: Jessica Thompson
www.Jessica.ie

Foreword by: Bill Bartmann

Cover Art by: Sam and Bax

# Table of Contents

# Dedications

### Jim

*To my wife, Allison, who has lived the crazy stories in this book with me. You are the best thing to ever happen to me. My daughters, Justine and Natalie, who not only make me very proud but also give me the drive to continue these crazy stories.*

*The great Frank McKinney, Mark Evans D.M., Doug Doebler and Vince Parrucci. Great to have you guys on the Batphone. My Super Attorneys; Matt Nichols and Matt "the debt Doctor" Herron. You guys are Rock Stars! Sue and Chuck from Scottsdale Studios who play a big part in creating the magic.*

*And last but not least...John Mulry, otherwise known as...The Irishman. Let's make some history!*

### John:

*To Jess – you're my everything, thanks for your love and support and your constant encouragement. To my clients and customers – keep taking action, keep moving forward and NEVER expect anything other than success.*

*To Jim, for great adventures thus far and the many more to come.*

# Foreword

Small business is the lifeblood of every economy. The entrepreneurs of the last 200 years forged a path that led America to the Super Power status it still holds today.

Yes, business is serious business. Very serious. I know a bit of what I speak of as I myself came from very humble beginnings.

As a teenager I was homeless and eating out of a dumpster. I was an alcoholic and paraplegic at eighteen after falling down a set of stairs drunk.

Yet, I walked out of that hospital and I set my sights on something bigger than homelessness and gang activity.

I put myself through College, started a small business, and then the following...

- Voted National Entrepreneur of the year

- Nominated for the Nobel Peace Prize

- Borrowed 3.1 Billion dollars from 120 different lenders for privately held startup companies

- Named one of the top 100 entrepreneurs of that last 100 years

- Made the Forbes 400 list

- And, I became a Billionaire...then lost is all, in 72 hrs. And now, I am well on my way to getting it back.

So you see, I do know business, very, very well.

My friend, Jim Toner, has written a book with John Mulry that could prove priceless for you and your business.

The gap between businesses using academia approaches and a real-world, proven, hard-earned approach is monumental.

Jim falls into the "been there, done that, got the T-shirt" category. He, just as I have, has been down, up, down, and back up again. I can assure you that the lessons learned on that journey are extremely valuable.

As you can see from their bios, both Jim and John are more than a proven commodity and does not rest on past accomplishments.

In this book, you will find not only great strategies, but also brutal honesty.

I have found that all too often in business people do not want to face the realities of the situation at hand.

With them, you will have no choice. They can be blunt, to the point and at times, irreverent. But most importantly, they speak the truth.

Read this book. Soak it all in and take it to heart. You have a very valuable asset in your hands.

~Bill Bartmann
BillBartmann.com

# Preface

*I'm Winston Wolf...I solve problems.*

—Pulp Fiction, 1994

 I love that quote.  For those of you who have not seen the movie, Winston Wolf is someone who is called in to clean up a BIG mess.  He is the problem solver of *all* problem solvers.

 For those of you who have seen it....well, no explanation needed.  When I initially wrote the first version of this book a few years back, the Winston Wolf character was my inspiration.  I had gone through so many ups and downs in business that I knew with every fiber of my being that I could help existing or new business owners and entrepreneurs with their problems.

 Things however, evolve, as they should.  As time passed I not only honed my skills I had begun to make some world class contacts that I knew would be a fit for the vision I had in mind which was not just helping entrepreneurs with business growth, but solving business PROBLEMS.

**Business problems.**

You may feel that you don't have any, but I beg to differ.

You *do* have problems. Some you may be ignoring. Some you may not see coming. And some that you know are there, but have no idea what to do about them.

That is where the Wolves come in. More on that later.

If you are currently a business owner or someone who is thinking about becoming a business owner, this book is for you. I will go so far as to say, *you NEED this book*.

---

### Why Write This Book?

So, what are my reasons for writing this book? Why would I have an interest in helping business owners? I have my own business to deal with, right?

Let me tell you that one of the major reasons for this book is due to my belief in entrepreneurship and small business. Those two things are the backbone of this country. Without those, we are doomed. I don't like the idea of being doomed.

I want you to read this book as if I am talking specifically to you, like we're sitting down having a beer together. This is straight talk to a friend.

I have been an entrepreneur for almost thirty years, and a professional real estate investor for just about twenty-five of those years. I have, as they say, "seen it all." What I see now is causing me a great deal of concern...concern because it is contributing to the destruction of many small business owners and entrepreneurs.

---

## Accurate Thinking

What's causing my concern?

The lack of accurate thinking!

Society has become so inundated with FAKE...that it alters people's perceptions. From the internet to social media to the real media . . . and I use that term loosely, we are pushed further and further away from the true reality of what it takes to become successful.

As a business owner/entrepreneur, you cannot afford to get caught in this trap. You need to be very aware of where you are at any given time in your business.

This book is about **REALITY . . .**

In my opinion, there is nothing that takes the place of entrepreneurship and being your own boss.

Nothing!

The ability to have total control over every aspect of your life is a very, very nice perk. But the perks are just the byproducts of running a successful business.

## The key word here is *Successful.*

This book is about what it takes to get there.

Yes, being a business owner is one of the greatest, most gratifying ventures you will ever undertake. But the *reality* is that there will not just be obstacles along the way, but roadblocks and pipe bombs too.

There will be *lots* of them.

You must learn how to successfully deal with and/or negate their impact on you and your bottom line.

After reading halfway through this book you might feel that you have mistakenly picked up a horror novel because some of what you read will, and should, scare you. That however, can be a good thing. It will either wake you up to correcting an existing problem, or help you prevent an oncoming one.

These problems, many of which you don't even know to expect, are far reaching: from employees, to marketing, to cash flow, to partners, to attorneys, and CPAs, to government interference, vendors, competitors, etc. The list goes on and on.

### Oh, by the way, you'll love the part about government interference.

(Just don't read it in the dark all alone.)

My point is this. It is called "business" for a reason. There are certain realities that you must confront in order to have a successful career as a business owner.

I know what I am talking about.

I have built multiple million dollar-plus businesses. As a result, I've been through:

- Employee issues
- Partner issues
- Government issues
- Cash flow issues
- Super highs and super lows

I have also seen very successful businesses destroyed overnight by refusing to acknowledge some of the topics in this book.

Yes, there are very real issues that you will encounter. And when you do, you need to know how to react. There is no shortage of namby-pamby advice available to you from management books with authors who have lots of letters after their name, as if this is some sort of reliable set of keys to the kingdom.

I am not knocking all the advice out there.

Admittedly, many of these people are far more book smart than I will ever be. But we are not talking about being book smart, are we? We are talking about *your* bottom line, and theory just doesn't cut it.

You will find no new age philosophy in this book.

What you will find is truth.

I know what I am talking about. I have friends and mentors who are mega-millionaires and even one who is a billionaire.

I have seen unprecedented success along with unimaginable failure. I have seen the "most likely to fail," succeed and "the most likely to succeed," fail.

I have gone from nothing more than a high school graduate to appearing on CNN, FOX, ABC, NBC, CBS, business journals, and national radio programs. I have taught thousands across the country how to create financial freedom through real estate investment as well as working with struggling business owners and getting them on the track towards huge profits and peace of mind.

I have been, and I am still, in the trenches. I not only live it, I am passionate about it! There is nothing that makes me happier that someone with the guts to step out on their own and go for it!

### *They grab life by the throat and scream, GIVE ME WHAT I WANT!!!*

This is what has made America great . . . people like you who have ventured into the unknown in hopes of creating a better life for yourself and your family.

And it is because of my passion for people like you, that I feel very protective.

I see on a daily basis how hard working business owners are being taken advantage of and I want to help…I

CAN help. I speak from hard-earned experience and I have the scars to prove it.

The goal with this book is to arm you to the teeth with hard-earned wisdom, resources, and inspiration needed in order to succeed AND make TONS of money, on your terms. You see, you will pay a price for your success. Win or lose, everybody pays, so let's make your price seem like the deal of the century.

So if you're ready to take this ride, all I ask of you is to LISTEN to both myself and John. Do not be so foolish as to think you can figure this out on your own. Learn from others mistakes as all successful people do. Should you choose to ignore our advice, well . . .

You'll see what happens then . . .

---

## Note to Newbie's

We wrote this book as if you are already in the game. That being said, some of you may be contemplating getting into the game so we want to make sure you are aware of what you are getting into.

Let's get right to the point here. There is no half way.

When you have made the decision to be a business owner, or continue to be a business owner/entrepreneur, you must adhere to the advice of Yoda:

*"Do, or do not. There is no try."*

He is correct...

There is no try.

It's sometimes hard to explain, this "entrepreneur" thing. I guess the best way to describe it is a "knowing", that you are different. A knowing that there is something better out there for you. A knowing that you are not like everyone else, and you will not settle for what it is everyone else settles for.

You just know.

---

## Warning #1

Now here is the first of our many warnings you will find throughout this book. If you DON'T know if this is the life for you and are just "kicking around the idea" or you want to dabble in a business enterprise to just "see how it works out," let me save you lots of time, money and heartache.

DON'T DO IT!

It's not for you. As I said, there is no half way. You don't dip your toes in the water. You jump in off the deep end.

One of the primary reasons for becoming an entrepreneur or business owner is MONEY. Let's be honest . . . it IS about the money.

Lots of money.

When you are talking about making lots of money, you also have to include the price you will pay for that money. No, it does not come free. As a matter of fact, the price can be high . . . sometimes too high for many to pay.

If you are not willing to go all out, all day, every day, this is not the path for you. This is a game of daily battles that must be fought and won in order to continue. And if you're not up for daily battles, you're not up for it at all.

Period.

My friend, the great Les Brown has a perfect quote:

*Life is a daily battle for territory.*
*Once you stop fighting for what you want,*
*what you **don't** want, automatically takes its place.*

19

Think on that one for a bit. "A *daily* battle for territory."

You need to answer this question for yourself. Are you willing to fight this battle? Are you willing to get kicked in the teeth and beaten down only to get back up again and say . . . bring it on?

Are you?

Now this is one of those, "Come to Jesus moments," where you need to be VERY honest with yourself. Can you take the hit? If you are already an entrepreneur, can you continue to take the hits?

They keep coming and they come from all directions.

They come from friends, family members, co-workers, media, government and even other so-called entrepreneurs. The biggest enemy you will face however . . . is YOU!

Yes, you.

That ever-present voice in your head that says you:

- Are not qualified
- Are not smart enough
- Don't have enough money
- Don't have enough skills

- Don't have enough connections, experience, etc., etc., etc.

This is why Les Brown said what he did. A *daily* battle for territory.

I can now see heads nodding in agreement as well as people putting down the book saying entrepreneurship is not for them.

It is what it is.

So for those of you who are still reading, great, you're in for some tough lessons, but they'll make you far more successful. Let's assume that you do want this life and you are willing to take the hit, or are willing to continue taking the hits. You're now asking, "How do I fight these battles?"

All battles must have a battle plan and in all battles you must know your enemy. And once the enemy has been identified, you can fight.

As I mentioned, the biggest and most constant battle will be fought with yourself. It comes in the form of the voice in your head that creeps in from time to time and tells you to throw in the towel. It whispers, "This battle will never end."

No matter how successful you become, at some point, doubt will creep in, which is why you must always be sharpening your sword.

---

**Remember This:**

- *If you worry about what others think, you will fail.*
- *If you think you're not good enough, you will fail.*
- *If you cannot convince yourself you ARE good enough, you will fail.*
- *If you are afraid of failure, you will fail.*
- *If you are not prepared to do what others will not, you will fail.*

---

**Good News**

Listen, there is good news. If you think that the accumulation of money has anything to do with anything other than a decision, then put this book back on the shelf now. You will not make it, because the truth is . . .

Money does not care who gets it!

Money does not discriminate. Money does not care if you are black or white or short or fat or ugly or handsome.

22

Money goes to those who attract it through their thoughts and actions. Money is neutral and will go to those who decide to get it.

That was a big clue there.

Money goes to those who decide . . . not hope for or think about . . . *DECIDE*.

Success is nothing more than a decision. You cut off all possibilities other that the path that leads to your goal. Ok, that was the good news. If you're ugly you still got a shot.

Enemy number one, which is you, has been identified.

---

**Bad News**

Who's next?

Look around, the enemy is everywhere. If I had to start somewhere it would be with the legion of "well meaning" people in your life who are more than willing to give you a daily beat down.

I call these people the "walking dead."

No affiliation to the TV show, but by the looks of some of them, you would never know. They have that grey, dead look about them; that look, by the way, comes from working a job you hate, for an unsatisfactory paycheck, and enough stress to choke a horse. They hate their life, and they know it. They are addicted to steady paychecks and perceived security like a junkie to crack.

They do, however, want to tell you how foolish you are to consider such a venture, or to continue chasing a stupid dream. They try to persuade you with their impassioned questions, "Wouldn't you rather have the security of a real job with two weeks paid vacation?"

Yeah, and for that real job security, you have to sit in traffic every day, go to a job you hate for an unsatisfactory paycheck. But hey, you should do it because it's what everybody does.

That says it all right there.

They want you to be like them. They want you to stay in their group. I mean really, if you get out and make it, what will it say about them?

They want you to fail . . . for them. It is their hang-up they're afraid of, and they're putting that burden, that expectation on you.

- *They will tell you all the horror stories of failed businesses.*
- *They will tell you how bad the economy is.*

- *They will tell you there is too much competition and that you can't do it.*

They want your soul. They want you to throw in the towel on your dream just as they did. They want you to be weak.

Adding insult to injury, the media hits you with a constant barrage of negativity and class warfare. They have TV shows devoted to the rich and famous. Something that you will never be is the underlying message. As a consolation prize however, you can watch someone else live his or her dreams on TV. And if it's on TV, it's got to be real, right?

The lists of those people or mediums that are looking to keep you down are endless.

I don't want to be overly dramatic but, this is war! You must have a strong belief in yourself and your goal. You need to be persistent. Not bull-headed, not unwilling to adjust course.

Persistent.

You need to trust your gut instincts. This is an invaluable tool that is too often ignored. Do not ignore it. You have gut instinct for a reason.

You need to continually learn and adjust. The minute you think you've "made it" and you stop doing what brought you to the dance, you will find yourself in a death spiral. Don't ignore me on this one, keep working on YOU!

## Life Isn't Fair

Above all else you need to remember that life is not fair. No one ever said it was. No one ever said it would be easy. Everybody pays. Rich, poor, young, old. Everybody. As an entrepreneur sometimes it seems that you may be paying more than your fair share. I get it, I've been there, but that's the game, and it's what you signed up for.

You need to keep your prospective when you're getting piled on.

Ask the kid in Haiti who hasn't eaten in a week about fairness. Ask the mother who just lost a child about fairness. Ask a promising young athlete who just became a quadriplegic about fairness. No, life is not fair, and neither is business.

It can be cold, cutthroat, and dirty.

But the payoff should you succeed? Not just the money. Your life, your soul, the power to control every part of your life.

This power to run your life the way you see fit is the real payoff.

You run the show. Yeah, you take the hits, but you also get the glory. You get the "knowing" that you weren't just one of the mindless masses being controlled to do the bidding of others.

I can assure you that there is great satisfaction in standing tall, bloody but unbowed. Knowing that you understood that we get one shot on this earth and you had the guts to take it. To be honest, sometimes that is even better than the money.

But we'll still take the money.

We always take the money.

So now that you are primed and ready to go, I am going to break this down into what I feel are the most important things you need to know in order to succeed.

## *NONE OF THIS IS THEORY*

You may not like much of what we have to say. You may even ignore what we have to say. I will caution you against this approach. Don't fall into the trap of thinking;

*"My business is different, so it doesn't apply."*

No, it's not.

We are all in the same business and you are not immune to what lurks in the shadows.

By reading all the way through this book, you will receive some very valuable insights on how to not only protect yourself, but how to **POSITION** yourself in the market place.

You may also be very surprised how obvious some of this advice is. My question, then, to you is:

## *"If it is so bleeping obvious, why are you not following it?"*

It is not good enough just to "know" something. You need to implement.

Everything in this book requires implementation. If that sounds like a lot of work, look at it this way: everything you implement will either *save*, or *make* you lots of money.

So back in the beginning I mentioned "evolution."

There is an old saying that goes, "No Man Is An Island" Though this book started as an "island" i.e. solo project, I found some people that were just too valuable to pass up.

My Co-Author in this book is one of the world's top marketers and his name is John Mulry. John is from Galway Ireland. Yup, I live in Scottsdale AZ and my fellow Wolf is in Galway Ireland. One of the things you are going to learn in this book is that BUSINESS HAS NO BOUNDARIES.

John brought something to the table that was even more valuable than his off the charts marketing and business strategies. He brought what I call, THE ATTITUDE. I'm not talking about a positive attitude or a "go get em" attitude; I'm talking about THE attitude of the Wolf. If this sounds silly to you, you are WAY off base. The Winston Wolf Pulp Fiction character on which the original edition of this book was going to be based was a solo act. A LONE WOLF if you will.

When you look at a Wolf pack however, they have built it traits and tendencies that have allowed them to survive and thrive for thousands of years. MANY of those same strategies go hand and glove with business. The funny thing is that not many people have seemed to catch it.

There are 2 sides to the Wolf. The one side is the fearsome creature that can rip you to shreds if needed. The other side is the one with the loyalty, the communication skills, and the strategies that have enabled it to be the legend that it is. John Mulry sees it as do I. When you are finished, you will also.

# We're a DIFFERENT Breed of Animal...

I'm a systems kind of guy. Maybe it's my mathematics and economics background (long story) but I believe in building systems in my business.

One's where you do the work once and you can benefit from them again and again.

In terms of your business you SHOULD view your marketing and advertising as systems.

Do the hard work once to build a machine that generates leads, encourages the most qualified to put their hands up and then converts them into clients.

The how you go about building these systems for your business will come later but I wanted to share with this with you because it was because of one of my systems that I came to meeting Jim.

You see, (and I'm sure you'd fit this bill to) Jim is a specific type of business owner. He's the type of business owner that does what I call the 'trifecta' of business success.

I'll be covering this in more detail in later chapters but for now I'll give you a quick summary.

Jim Toner is the type of business owner that INVESTS in himself, he then CONSUMES what he invests in and then he ACTS on what he consumes.

When Jim started dusting himself off after the HELL he went through (there's a million dollar education in store for you when you read it) he started putting things in place to get back on top and one of the first steps he took was INVESTING in one of my programs, he then CONSUMED what he invested in and then ACTED upon what he consumed.

His actions led him to be introduced to me by way of one my many marketing funnels and he reached out to me and we immediately got on because we speak the same language, have the same values and ideals.

We began working together and have been ever since.

While working together Jim and I started sharing more and more of our personal history and while I believe my story is quite powerful and inspirational to many business owners it pales in comparison to what Jim has had to endure.

When we decided to write this book I pleaded with him to tell his story. He was reluctant at first but thankfully agreed. New business or old, fledgling or flourishing what you're about to read is one of the best business educations you'll ever get.

We learn and grow through stories, have done since the dawn of time and will do long after the machines 'take over'. Jim has gone through hell and back in business, but his heartache and pain is your gain because in sharing is story you get to benefit as if you went through it yourself.

Like Jim mentioned, a lot of what you're about to read in these pages will most likely have you shrieking, possibly even fuming but trust me, we don't say these things to scare you, but to instill you with the accurate truth about running your business.

Sugar coating is fine for kids but we're all adults here, I'll be the first to admit it, I'm not as blunt as Jim but then I haven't gone through the hell he has. He's still standing and in my books, when you go through hell and you come out the other side with you DRIVE to help other businesses intact, then that's the kind of person I want in my corner.

Brace yourself, be honest to yourself and take these hard truths with the solace that we're hitting you with them not to harm you but to help you.

I'll be back later on but for now, buckle your seat because you're about to get a MILLION DOLLAR education.

# The MILLION DOLLAR Education

I believe great stories have real value and they should be shared, no matter how ugly or painful. I also believe in the power of redemption and I know that is what many are looking for in their lives. I may or may not know you and likewise but that does not matter.

This is for everyone.

All my blood and guts on the table not for my benefit, but for yours. This is a world full of fake and I will show you real. This is sometimes a world of despair, and I will show you hope. I will go so far as to say that this may be life changing for some of you for no other reason other than you can see that even when stripped of everything, victory is still within reach.

Maybe the lifeline you didn't think was available is here in this post. Or it could be something as simple as realizing that you are not alone. Everyone has a battle.

This is the first time this story is being told and there are only a small handful of people that really know everything. You will not only know everything and you will gain ENORMOUS benefit from my experience.

It is safe to say that this will be a Million Dollar education for you…

For those without the patience to read all the blood and guts but want the end result? Feel free to jump ahead and come back to all the juicy details later. If you do make the jump, you will learn that the following will NOT kill you but make you stronger.

- Failed Business
- Dream Home lost
- Nasty Bankruptcy
- Family tragedy and death
- Relentless Government attacks
- Your money stolen and reputation smeared with lies
- Re-Starting from zero, with zero

Everything you will read is true even though it may seem unbelievable at times and much of it is embarrassing for me to write but I am absolutely convinced that I was put through this journey for a reason that may have nothing to do with me.

This journey was painful…very painful. It also was not quick. It began in 2008 and has still not ended. When I say it was a fight, it was a FIGHT, but that is what life and business is…a fight.

The storms come.

Sometimes it's one or sometimes it's many. In my case, it was 7 storms all at the same time. I wanted to share my experience because I see so many people that are just begging for that one piece of information or advice that can save them, but they can never find it, and they quit.

I spent my life training myself to get through the storm but I didn't realize I would have 7 dumped on me at once. Frankly, as I was going through it I don't think I really realized how I was doing it.

I remember before putting this book together I was talking with an old friend and told them the story. The look on their face said it all and they said, "How in the world did you get through that" And then, it hit me. It was very clear to me how I did it.

**I BECAME THE STORM**

# How A Wolf Came To Be

I am a barely high school graduate that had no special skills or talents to really do much of anything. All I knew was that I wanted to make money. I didn't care how I did it, as long as it was legal. A fate would have it one night 27 years ago; I was sucked into one of the "Get Rich In Real Estate" infomercials and was hooked.

I didn't necessarily buy into the "guru" but I did buy into the fact that people could make money investing in real estate. Back in those days I had A LOT of bad habits but one of the good ones I had was that I was a reader. I was fascinated by the rags to riches stories and how people made their money. One common thread in most of the stories I read was "Real Estate" They either made their money there or they had extensive real estate holdings. In other words, RICH PEOPLE HAD REAL ESTATE!

Since working three jobs and still not making it I decided to go for it. I bought the program, found and paid a mentor and within 30 days I had made almost $10,000 with no money and no credit. And I do mean, NO MON-EY and NO CREDIT.

That was all I needed to turn me into a deal making maniac. I was off and running and making more money than I ever dreamed of making. Slowly as time passed and my successes grew, people began asking, "How do you do that real estate stuff"? So, I taught a few people and it worked out well. Eventually, my partner and I decided to form a Coaching Company teaching LOCAL people what we did. And that is when the rocket ship took off.

If you are interested in the entire, fully detailed story you can read about it in my Consumers Guide to Investment Real Estate.

The year is 2008. My Real Estate Investment training Company, Jim Toner's Wealth Builders was going in full swing. We had created enormous success teaching local people how to legitimately make money with investment real estate. This was not the "get rich in real estate" info-mercial stuff, this was real. Between myself and my core team we had over 100 years of active investing experience between us so we knew our stuff and we got results.

We also had the advantage of being in Pittsburgh Pa, which was and still is one of the best and safest real estate markets in the Country. Personally, I was killing it. I was making over $800,000 a year, had a Million Dollar home, an $80,000 car, and lots of money in the bank and lots of fans. We did things the right way and people appreciated it.

I was even written up in the Pittsburgh Business Times for my successes as well as having appeared on National News for giving away debt free homes to returning veterans. Things were great.

So what do you do when things are going great?

You expand. You go bigger. Go big or go home right? Actually, that was NOT the smart thing to do but that is what businesses think they should do. That one little mistake alone probably cost me $500,000. But, nonetheless…go big or go home.

I figured that since our concept of training local people to invest in real estate worked in Pittsburgh, it would work everywhere. I decided to open offices at a rapid pace. Akron, Columbus, Indianapolis… all at the same time and all which required tremendous cash outlay. In each City the monthly radio advertising alone was in the $15,000 - $25,000 range, all payable upfront. This did not include renting office space, seminar production and everything else involved in opening an office.

Nonetheless, I was convinced. This is what is known as, "victim of your own success" thinking. During this time the small rumblings of what would become a 10.0 Earth Quake began to pop up on the radar. Actually, they had been on the radar but I was ignoring the signs. Pittsburgh was such a strong investment market I ignored the bigger, global picture of what was coming.

Pay Attention to the signs…

By 2009 there was no way to ignore it. The Country was in the grips of a financial storm that likes of which had not been seen since the Great Depression. My real estate investment seminars went from having hundreds of people to having a dozen. People were paralyzed with fear and there was nothing I could do to change their mind. But, not being a quitter, I kept trying. Hint: "sometimes, you need to quit"

Eventually, after bleeding out six figures, I had to shut down the Ohio and Indy offices. An Attorney friend of mine STRONGLY recommended just walking and bankrupting the Company. I refused. I was brought up to pay your debts no matter what. So, I paid. Hint: Sometimes, you are foolish to pay"

I soon found myself back in my comfort zone of Pittsburgh. It was after all the BEST and SAFEST place to invest in real estate, I was very established and the City was not affected in any way by the financial crash. I was very excited by the possibilities for any would be investors as THIS, was the place to be. Invest in Pittsburgh now, and make a killing.

So, I spent money. Lots of money on marketing, seminars and even and infomercial attempting to capitalize on the crash which is EXACTLY when you should be trying to capitalize.

2010: Much to my dismay, my plan was not working. My enthusiasm could not overcome the panic people were feeling even though the City was not affected by the financial crisis.

Not only was I bleeding money at a frightening pace, the banks due to the crisis cut us off. Not just us either. Clients who were new investors were now unable to get loans to buy deals. Literally, lending criteria changed overnight and the ability to jump into the investment pool suddenly became VERY difficult. Even we were hit as out credit lines were called and canceled and getting loans for real estate deals became a no go even for me.

I was now being VERY strongly urged to get out, B.K. everything and walk away and live to fight another day. Again, I refused and things got worse. I was now using all my personal money trying to keep things going. I thought things were pretty grim until the day the fuse was lit on the bomb that was about to be dropped on me.

I don't remember the exact date, but I do remember the feeling of, "oh shit, this is going to get ugly" Enter Vince, one of my most trusted friends and employee at the time had been trying to tell me for some time that he was uneasy with my sales manager and he felt something was "off."

I ignored these warnings because the person in question was also a friend that I had known for years, but he was also my next-door neighbor. No way would he be up to anything underhanded. Vince however persisted. He came to me one day and said "Jim, at least look at the books so I can feel better" I said fine. The book in question was an account that said sales manager was also a signer. I was SO busy trying to keep things going that I completely ignored the "little things" that turned out to be "Big" things

So what did I find? All toll over $230,000 gone with over $100,000 in cash alone written in checks to HIM! It was also during this time that this person had decided to "work from home". I thought nothing of it until I realized WHY he didn't want to be in the office. I had been walking around blind but this opened my eyes very quickly.

I immediately called a good friend of mine who is a Cop and he set me up with a detective in the County. When I say this was outright theft, this was outright theft. We even had the canceled checks! It's an odd feeling when something like this happens. As mad as you are there is some part of you that wants to hope it is a mistake and that things can be worked out. I just didn't want to believe it. This was a friend, my neighbor...not some stranger. I was thrown for a loop but that was just the beginning.

Weeks passed and the detective got back to us and said, "yup, this guy is guilty as sin" "I'm going to set up a meeting with the prosecutors for you" Great...got em.

A few days later, Vince and I meet with the prosecutors and give them the story and evidence as well as the detective providing his findings. What happened next was the next kick in the teeth.

They shut the door and said to me, "look, we know he did it. The problem we have is that he is claiming you told him he could have the money and if we take this to trial and lose, it looks very bad at ELECTION TIME!"

Vince and I looked at each other in disbelief. I said, "Are you kidding me? Because it will look bad for re-election if you lose?" Yes he said. I'm sorry but we can't risk it. Sue him civilly and you will win. It is a slam-dunk. This was my first REAL WORLD experience with politics and it was ugly. I would soon find out how ugly it could really be.

It was now impossible to stop the bleeding of cash and I and my Company were on the ropes. I met with my Attorney and he uttered the words I did not want to hear. "Jim, you need to file bankruptcy and you need to do it now" He then proceeded to tell me that I made a major error by not doing it MUCH earlier.

Believe it or not, some people LOVE to file B.K. as do many businesses. It is after all a safety net provided by the Government to help you get back on our feet. I did not view it that way. I saw it as a total failure. The worst part, was telling my wife who stuck with me thru thick and thin. Believe me when I tell you that telling your spouse you need to file B.K. is not a pleasant conversation.

Understanding that we really did have no option, we decided to proceed. My Attorney, who is one of the best B.K lawyers in the Country, assured us that this would be quick and painless. As it turned out, it would be more accurate to say, VERY slow and agonizing death, which I will explain. But first, let's talk about another storm brewing.

CHAPTER **4**

---

# When it Rains,
# it Pours...

As I explained, the employee that stole the money from me was also a friend, AND neighbor. The person in question was very outgoing and it was VERY important to him that people thought he was the greatest. I didn't realize how far he took it until after the theft.

During our investigation we discovered that this person, who proudly proclaimed the was a big success even though he was only a high school grad had different profiles online. One showed he graduated and had a degree from the University of Pittsburgh. Another said he had a degree from Penn State. In truth, he really was just a high school grad. These profiles he created were simply to inflate people's view of him.

That was just to beginning of his smoke screen but it is not worth getting into the details. It became a running joke with all the dirt we found on him. Anyway, I think you get the point of what I was dealing with.

So, this person was now extremely alarmed that I was going to let the neighborhood know what he did. Although I was not very close with all the neighbors we did frequently get together for parties and our kids played together.

About one week after being told we needed to file a civil suit I began to notice very odd behavior in the neighborhood. People stopped waving at us and my kid's friends stopped calling. We decided to speak to one of the neighbors and that is when my wife and I were informed that the thief and already gone to everyone and told them that I was the one that stole the money and I was a criminal!

Now think about this. Myself and my Attorneys as well as law enforcement have ALL the proof in the world against him, including over 100k in canceled checks and he is telling people it was I? This was his desperate attempt to save his made up image.

My wife and I were stunned by this and told our side to this neighbor but we could tell she didn't believe us. She was far closer to him than to my wife and I as were the other neighbors. We chose not to even bother talking to the others and very quickly; we became the outcasts in the neighborhood. The hardest part was my kids being shunned. Nonetheless, we knew the truth and wanted no part of anyone that would believe such lies without even asking our side of the story.

Are we keeping score?

Business blows up. Employee steals over 200K. Bankruptcy unavoidable. Outcasts of the neighborhood. Ha! That's nothing...we are just getting started.

A Bankruptcy hearing is not much fun. Basically, you get in a room in front of a judge and most likely lots of creditors and are humiliated. Like I said, not fun. Mine was even less fun as the employee that stole my money showed up at the hearing with his Attorney to badger me into dropping my civil suit against him, as you cannot be suing someone if you are in B.K. Once again I am learning that Justice is not what I thought it was.

I also discovered that at least in my case, a B.K. was not an easy ride. Not to bore you with the details but my Attorney said that mine was the most invasive B.K. he had ever been a part of. He could not understand why they were putting me thru the ringer like they were and neither could I. Well, we found out one fine day when he got a call from the trustee informing him that due to a phone call from the thief's Attorney telling the trustee that I was "hiding" things and attempting fraud" they were going to REALLY look VERY closely at everything I had done in my business and personal life.

My Attorney actually pulled me aside one day and said, "Jim, is there something you are not telling me. I am your Attorney, you can tell me. I have never seen anything like this and the trustee said that if they find misconduct, they are going to recommend criminal charges"

I said, sorry, no dirt and I can clearly see what is happening. The thief needed to destroy me to hide what he had done. And so we continued…for almost 2 years. I had to provide documentation that my Attorney said was insane. Thank God we were good record keepers. He was even convinced that they were out to get us due to that well placed phone call.

Meanwhile, during this period the one saving grace my wife and I had was our home. We were going to be able to keep our home, which was our custom-built dream home. It was also a home that I had foolishly put close to 300K in cash into.

We had occasionally noticed that when it rained, pools would form in our back yard. At first we thought nothing of it but steadily things got worse. When bad rains came, our built in pool would be flooded with mulch from the landscape, which resulted in a $300.00 pool-cleaning bill each time.

Then came the day when the water made its way into my basement. Now, this was not any basement. The was a $150,000 custom basement. I'm talking custom bar, woodwork, you name it. Yup, big money can make you do stupid things.

Back to the water. This was a pretty concerning event as I had laid out a big chunk of money and this was the one thing we could keep in the B.K. I contacted an engineering company to come out and see if they could determine what was causing the problem.

The good news is that they did a VERY thorough investigation. The bad news is what they came back to me with. They informed that I basically had 2 BIG problems. The first was the developers engineer, MISSED taking into account the 13 Acres behind my home that all drained into MY yard. Problem number 2...the builder, built the home too low. Basically, we were sitting in the bottom of a bowl and all the water was coming to us.

I was informed that IF it could be corrected at all, it would be a VERY expensive fix. Upwards of $100,000.

Unsure of what to do I contacted the developer, who was also a friend, AND lived in the neighborhood. I reported to him the findings and inquired about how to remedy the situation. After all, his engineer made a monumental error.

Would you like to venture a guess as to his answer? Now this is a guy I had known for 15 years and someone that sat on the board of our charitable foundation. He said, "sorry Jim, there is nothing I can do"

A punch is the gut would be an understatement. Here I am going through the worst time of my life and the one thing my family has to hold onto is our home and my "friend" turns his back.

I had no choice but to contact a law firm who specialized in these kinds of cases and they were even shocked. Apparently it is pretty rare to 2 major errors such as these to happen on the same property. We filed suit against the builder and the developer who decided to "tag team" me and work together.

The builder actually had the balls to say that because we signed off on the final grading they were off the hook. The home was built too low but the final grading saves them?

Months progressed and the developer and builder dug their heels in knowing that I was in financial straits. They were right. My Attorneys were confident we would win but it would take time and I would be looking at a massive legal bill. I couldn't do it. I was in the middle of a B.K. and I was tapped.

Within weeks after walking from the suit, a massive rainstorm completely flooded and destroyed the entire basement.

Often times in life you are given signs. For my family and me, it seemed like we were going to be given signs until we got the message. The message finally came in the form of my wife's mom entering the early stages of Alzheimer's. I really can't think of a more wicked disease. My in-laws lived in Scottsdale AZ and they were basically alone out there. We also knew things would get worse with her at a rapid pace.

What we did next was something extremely important in times of crisis...we drank. No, just kidding. We took an accurate assessment of where we really were standing.

**And, we drank.**

Here is how the picture looked.

- The business was gone

- We were in the middle of a nasty B.K.

- Our home was being destroyed and was now worthless to us.

- The neighbors believed we were criminals and I was forced to live next door to the real criminal

- My children were blackballed in the neighborhood.

- My mother in law has been diagnosed with Alzheimer's.

I had luckily brainwashed myself with enough rags to riches stories that I knew storms come into everyone's life. I just didn't think it would be so many at one time. So what do you do when storms come? Find better weather. I said to my wife, "someone is sending us a sign that we need to leave this place. Let's go to Arizona and help take care of your mom and start over."

On the surface that sounds pretty good. New place, great weather etc. In reality, it was a very difficult decision. We basically had to pick our lives and leave everything behind, and start all over. My daughters were crushed and I felt like we were being run out of town. I knew however that there was no other decision to make. Many times in life you will find that the most difficult decisions to make are the very best ones to make. Still, it is not easy.

During times like these it is very easy to take your eye off the ball and lose sight of the bigger picture. The reality is that no matter how bad the situation, life goes on and you need to be prepared for tomorrow...literally, tomorrow. I think this is where my years of reading and studying success AND failure stories helped me remain somewhat clear during a time that it would have been very easy to crumble.

My plan to pick and leave to Arizona was agreed upon but as I said, what about tomorrow? The first thing I needed to do was find a place to live and coming from what once was a beautiful dream home I was none too anxious to move into a tiny apartment in a shitty neighborhood. This ordeal literally stripped me of our home, money and even car. We were really starting at zero. There was one thing however that was not taken and could not be taken and that was my skill as an entrepreneur and real estate investor.

SOMETHING WEIRD. I know that all the above and all of what is coming sounds very scary and bad...BUT...something weird seemed to happen during these challenges. We STILL had fun! We had good friends, had good times and life went on. We also started to feel a little...bulletproof? Weird, I know, but remember, there is no dark without light.

I knew that good things are always around you, it's just that sometimes you need to look a little harder.

CHAPTER 5

---

# Adversity Carries Seeds of Opportunity...

There is an old saying that you could take all a million-aires money and in a very short time he or she would have it all back is true. The skills remain.

My wife and I decided that we would not settle. It took some coaxing from me because she was obviously very scared but I convinced her that we would find a great place at a great price. Now remember, we are back to no money, no credit...

What did I do? Simple...I jumped in the way back machine and fell back on the skills that built me up in the first place. I understood that Scottsdale AZ, the area we were headed to was one of the hardest hit areas in the Country during the real estate crash. I also knew that meant desperate owners that were also looking to make a deal.

It is SO important to remember that when you are going through a wipe out, you are NOT alone.  It is so easy to feel like you and only you are the biggest failure in the world and everyone else is just kicking back and living large.  NOT TRUE.  Keep your eyes on the ball and always look for the opportunity.

With the help of my sister-in-law we found a beautiful 3,200 sq. ft. home in one of the most exclusive areas of Scottsdale for only $2,100 a month.  That may sound like a lot of money to some and it was to me at the time, but this is a home that would normally go for close to $4,000.  I could not settle for going to rock bottom.  This was not because I felt I was too good to live in a modest home in a modest area but more the fact that I knew I could not afford the MENTAL cost of such a backwards move.  I was willing to concede on some things, but not everything.

For those wondering how we got such a deal?  Simple.  Desperate owner that could not pay their mortgage.  They didn't care that we just filed a B.K. and had no credit.  Their only concern was that we would pay the rent.

What did I concede on?  Well, I went from driving an $80,000 BMW to a 2004 Chevy Impala that my wives brother kindly gave to us.  I figured, "what the hell" I'm not a big car guy anyway and no one here knows me so why not.  For a SHORT period you CAN swallow a few bitter pills as long as you don't make a habit of it or more importantly, become comfortable with it.

Rebuild time. We arrived in AZ in the middle of summer and needed to put a full court press on getting things back on track. Did I mention it is HOT in the AZ desert in the summer? It is not only hot, but the desert for all its beauty is very unforgiving. It has a way of very clearly making you understand that there is a way to survive and there is a way to die...your choice.

The choice for me was easy, but that doesn't mean the road will be. It was my wife's role to make sure the kids got acclimated in our new town and also to begin with taking care of her mom who was getting progressively worse. By the time we got there she really didn't remember any of us. Our Bankruptcy was also still going on. I think they were trying to set a new world record with us.

My job was to work on not just getting our life back, but getting it back in the way WE wanted. We had taken a very big financial and personal hit and I did not like it. I found myself in an interesting position. Here I was in a new town, no connections, no money or credit and I had to get things moving lickety split. There was no time for down time.

One of the cool things about the desert is that no matter how Type A you may be, it has a way of bringing back your focus. The desert offers not many distractions and it is pretty easy to THINK without being pulled in a million different directions.

Here was the conversation I was having with the desert shortly after our arrival.

"So Jim, here we are. You now have to do what you teach people to do. Your claim to fame was becoming a successful investor with no money and no credit. You have told the story to and taught thousands your strategies. Now it is YOU who are the one that has to perform. Not only is it you that is on the line, you need to do it with nothing but your wits. New Town, no connections, no money, no nothing. Let's see what you are really made of"

Honest to God, that was the conversation I was having with myself and not just once. My biggest complaints against the "make money in real estate" industry are the frauds that are prevalent in the industry.

## CHAPTER 6

---

# Dance with the one that brought you to the dance...

I can tell you for a fact that most of the well-known "guru's" are not even investors and some are outright frauds. The get away with it due to huge financial backers that allow them to spend BIG money on marketing and smoke and mirrors that deceive the public. I had always prided myself as being a "Real" investor and now I had to prove it again. Not to the public...to ME.

There is an old saying, "dance with the one that brought you to the dance" What brought me to the dance was making deals. I had a knack for finding deals and making money off of them...often, with no money and no credit.

I also had a knack for connecting with the public. I was and am as real as it comes and it really resonates with a public that is desperately searching for something "Real" that they can sink their teeth into.

Having done some prior business in California and having a few connections there I was contemplating the idea of doing some seminars. Like the AZ market, the California market got hit very hard by the downturn and I knew there were good opportunities to be had. I pulled together a few partners and I began doing radio in Sacramento California. I was following the same formula that had worked for me all those years in Pittsburgh, which was speaking about opportunity, and telling the truth be it good or bad.

It was slow going at first with people still being shell shocked by the crash. I remember my first seminar in Sacramento had only about 14 people in attendance and I told them emphatically, "if you buy NOW, in 2 years you will be jumping for joy"

Out of those 14, there were 2 people who became clients and took my advice. Today, they are jumping for joy. Fear cannot only be crippling, it can lead you to be blind to the enormous opportunities right in front of you.

Also during this time I began writing the first edition on my Consumers Guide To Investment Real Estate. For those who have it, no explanation needed. For those who don't, it was just a basic outline of how to get started in the business. More importantly however were the stories from everyday people that followed those strategies and their results.

If you don't have a copy, you can get the updated version at www.creating101.com

All in all, things were going good on the business front as it didn't take me long at all to get back into doing deals in Cali and Arizona as well. We were still however dealing with the Bankruptcy almost 18 months into it. As stated earlier, my Attorney had never seen anything like it and he made this point to the judge.

Nonetheless, they were putting me thru the ringer and they would decide IF, WHEN and HOW this would end. Believe me when I tell you that you really need to keep focus on MOVING FORWARD when going thru something like this. When you go through your days knowing that the Feds are on you is not fun. I knew that I not only did nothing wrong but went over and above trying to avoid a B.K. so I felt confident.

Days here in the desert often run together due to the great weather. It's kind of like every day is the same and sometimes you don't even remember what you did the day before.

One day however REALLY stood out to me.

## CHAPTER 7

# "Oh Look, Here Comes the Wealth Builder"

I opened my mailbox that fateful day in 2013 and saw a letter from the Pennsylvania Attorney General's Office. Apparently someone had filed a complaint against my Company and being the owner, they wanted to have a little conversation with me.

Now I am not easily flustered but with everything I was dealing with, this was not something I was happy to see. I am a guy that has never even gotten a traffic ticket so I was pretty taken aback. What was even crazier was what they were asking for.

They wanted me to provide EVERYTHING I EVER DID in my business from 2001 to current day. All my radio ads, training materials, copies of websites, AND they wanted my entire database with all names and contact info of anyone who had even gone to one of my seminars.

Me, still being nice guy Jim, knowing I did nothing wrong made the mistake of picking up the phone and calling them. I was told that this "was no big deal" and they just had a few questions about a past client. They also said, "this is very informal...no need to bring an Attorney"

That my friend is what we call a RED FLAG! First of all, asking me for everything my business ever did IS a big deal. Telling me not to bring an Attorney? Well, they just showed their hand.

I knew I had to be smart about this as I have heard horror stories of what the Government can and will do if they want you. One of my good friends, and former Billionaire, Bill Bartmann, had the U.S. Government falsely accuse him of multiple securities violations and hit him with enough felony counts that he was facing almost 300 years in prison! He fought them, and he won.

The cost however was it took him form Billionaire to bankrupt and over 3,500 people that worked for him losing their jobs. He received a letter of apology from the Government for his troubles.

So, my next call was to an Attorney, and a good one. This was not what I wanted or needed to spend money on at the time but I had no options. The next call I made was even dumber that the one where I called the A.G.

I put in a call to one of my best friends since childhood who happened to be a very successful client of mine, AND, he worked for the A.G's office in the Narcotics division. I asked if what this letter meant as I have never even gotten a traffic ticket.

He said he would look into it right away for me. Big mistake. Stay tuned for details on why.

So I book a flight to Pittsburgh, meet with my Attorney and head off to our "meeting" with the Deputy A.G. When I say the experience was surreal, I mean it was surreal. We walked in the door of their office and myself and my Attorney hear 2 employees in a VERY mocking tone say, *"oh look, here comes the Wealth Builder"*

I turned to him and said, *"Did you just hear that?"* He was as shocked as I was and I knew right away that I had obviously been to topic of discussion and that I was clearly the enemy to them.

The next hour was a VERY clear example as to why a very large portion of the American public despises the Government. First off, it had gotten back to this person that my buddy had been asking around and that made her very angry. In her mind, I was CLEARLY guilty of something and was trying to use my influence to get this squashed. The truth was, I was only asking a friend what it was I received.

The complaint in question was from a client that I did not even know who purchased a program from the sales manager that worked for me. Yes, THAT sales manager.

The contract was EXPIRED for over 2 years and according to our records, the person in question made no attempts to live up to his end of the deal. We also found out later that this person called the A.G. and told them that "Someone who claims to be a Wealth Builder is in Bankruptcy"

I want to be very blunt with this next statement. I know a lot about success and what it takes to get there. Contrary to what all the "guru's" say, it is not easy. It is VERY doable, but not easy. One of the most important traits you need to have is PERSONAL RESPONSIBILITY. The truth is, YOU, will be the reason for your success and failure and finger pointing only sets you back farther.

This person who filed this complaint chose to blame rather than accept responsibility. Not only that, they chose to totally ignore any legality of a contract, which shows lack of character.

Imagine if you went to College. I never did but for the analogy. You went to College, didn't do YOUR part and when you didn't get a good job upon leaving, you decide not to pay your school loans and just say, "it didn't work" "I am not going to pay and I want my money back"

This person chose to go to an EXTREME measure, without even talking with me and chose to try and wreck my life. As I said, I don't even know this person, but I can assure you 100% they will NEVER reach any level of success in their life.

Our "meeting" was to say the less, "interesting". My Attorney and I were basically told that not only do contracts NOT MATTER, and that the A.G's office does not have a statute of limitation, we were told that basically everything real estate investors do is illegal. This is the classic Government/ Corporate vs. Entrepreneur mentality.

Now obviously none of what she was asserting is true but this is a very important lesson you need to understand especially if you are a business owner. When dealing with the Government on issues like this, the truth is RARELY relevant. Please re-read that last sentence.

The other thing you need to understand is that this is all about money and politics. Remember earlier when I referenced my first experience with how the legal / political system worked?

Well, here I am on the other end of the situation and it was clear that I was going to be used to further someone else's career.

We left the meeting with my Attorney not overly concerned but with me being very concerned. I am very good at reading people and it was clear as day that I was looked down upon because I was an Entrepreneur.

We agreed to cooperate and provide some additional information they requested, as we knew we had the law on our side and had done nothing wrong. In hindsight, all that did was make things worse.

CHAPTER **8**

# The FEDS and the BIG Fish...

Meanwhile, back at the ranch.... Merry Christmas! Not literally but it sure felt like it when I FINALLY got the call from my Attorney that my Bankruptcy had been discharged! It was over and I passed with flying colors.

My Attorney only half jokingly said this should have been a case study. It was a very long and hard emotional and financial road but it was over and my family could now move forward without this hanging over our heads...or so we thought.

As I continued to re-build my business and my life the A.G's office in Pennsylvania continued on a bizarre and frightening search for some type of smoking gun although neither I nor my Attorney had any clue as to what it could be.

It seemed the more we cooperated the more they turned the screws. One day I received a call from a client that informed me they had received a call from someone at the A.G's office informing them that I had filed a bankruptcy and asked if they would "like to complain" about anything.

They did not get the answer they were hoping for as number 1 telling them I had filed a B.K. and number 2 in their opinion, attempting to coerce them into saying something bad about me, appalled this client.

As time went on, I began to get more calls from more clients telling me the same thing and also reacting the same way, with disgust.

Shortly after theses calls began, we were contacted by the A.G. and told that they wanted me to submit my entire database of names and contacts. My Attorney laughed and said, "why, so you can start calling people and try and get them to complain?' To our dismay, she said, "YES"

Our answer...nope, get a court order. That was the end of that conversation, as they knew that would never happen.

Then came the really fun phone calls. Once again, one of my clients contacted me and said *"Jim, the FBI wants to talk to me about you"* Yes, the FBI.

Now, pay CLOSE attention here. If God forbid you should ever find yourself in a position like this your response needs to be what my response was. My response, "Thanks for the call but if they contacted you I cannot and will not have any conversation with you until it is done. Be helpful and forthcoming and I will talk with you when this is all over"

Once again, make sure you understand those last few lines. You CANNOT in any way shape of form be seen as attempting to interfere in any type of investigation with the FEDS. If you did nothing wrong and interfere, guess what, you just did something wrong. Stay out of it and let your Attorneys handle it.

I also received a call from my media buyer in California whom I had done Millions in dollars in business with telling me the she was called by the Security Exchange Commission regarding me and one of the people that worked for me. That phone call cost me the business relationship, as she was afraid she would need to get an Attorney and could not afford to do so and she cut ties with me.

To say my head was spinning at this point would be a HUGE understatement. It was becoming so bizarre, that I needed to do some digging myself and find out WHY this was happening and the motive behind it. My Attorneys were VERY calm and just kept saying, "don't worry about it, there is nothing there" I already knew that but it did not seem to matter.

Here is what I found out when I decided to start asking questions and doing my own research. When you work for the Attorney General's Office as an Attorney, you are essentially an employee that must be able to justify your job. That means, bring in money. The Attorney in question has been with the office since 2003. In 2007 she busted a legit bad guy in a mortgage fraud case and has done nothing of note since that case. It had been years since she had done anything of note and saw me as her ticket.

They LOOK FOR what they perceive to be BIG fish in order to gain public approval. I also found out from a prominent Attorney that they actually have quotas they need to meet as this is needed at guess when…ELECTION TIME. Remember when I could not get someone that stole form me arrested due to political reasons?

I was perceived as a "bad guy" in part due to the "make money in real estate" world, and truth be told, it is unfortunately a very bad industry. I wrote an entire chapter on how dirty it really is in my new Consumers Guide Book. You MUST read what I have uncovered.

I also found out that size matters. Sorry, couldn't resist. But seriously, it does. I could not understand how they were coming so hard after me but ignoring the BIG Companies out there that were really dong some bad things.

Here is what I was told. They came for me because they perceived me as weak and unable to fight back. The big Companies have Attorneys on staff and the A.G's office does not want to fight them due to budgetary reasons. It would take too long and odds are that they would lose anyway.

This was becoming so dirty that it was making me sick to my stomach. Go for the small businessman and make an example out of them whether they did anything or not.

As we continued down this hellhole, I was informed that, ready for this? I COULD NOT TALK TO MY CLIENTS! Yes, if you were a paying client I was not allowed to talk to you! In case you may be wondering why you have not heard from me in 4 years? Well, there you go. The Attorney in question was attempting to get me banned from ever doing business in the state if Pennsyl-vania again.

I think the A.G's office would be slightly alarmed if they knew how many of my clients want to form a lawsuit with me and go after them as they feel they have been hurt by not being allowed to work with me. That would not look good at guess when? Election time.

Oh, I forgot to mention. The Attorney General her-self was indictment on criminal charges and had her law license suspended. Yes, this is the person signing off on going after me. Someone with no legal ability to practice law, AND under criminal indictment. More on that later.

## CHAPTER 9

# Back to the Business World...

Listen, the best revenge against things like this is success and making money and that is where I was rapidly moving towards. I was very pleased at how fast I recovered which validated what I had been teaching people, which was you really could start with nothing and make it.

It has been beaten to death but attitude really is the key. Actually, it is Attitude, AND Strategy.

One real bright spot during this "storm" was reconnecting with a great guy that I had some dealings with in the past concerning real estate. His name is Gary but I call him Mr. Landlord. He lives in Akron Ohio and is the proud owner of over 157 single-family homes.

When I took a trip to Akron to see what Gary was doing he asked me if he could have an autographed copy of my book. I said, "Me? I want an autographed copy of YOUR book" He doesn't have one but he should and will if I have anything to do with it.

Akron turned out to be a gold mine I began doing deals there even before I got back to Arizona. Beautiful little single family homes, totally remodeled, rented and managed returning 12% - 15% with most having over $15,000 in equity. Not to mention the massive growth and turn around that was happening in the City.

Not only did I dive into the Ohio market but my California clients did also. In Sacramento they needed to spend $230,000 for a rental property. That math does NOT work.

I was very pleased that those California clients had chosen to not only listen to me, but also trust me. They didn't let the fear of not living where the deals were get in their way of a smart financial decision. Investment real estate is all about the math and sometimes, depending on where you live in the Country, the math just doesn't work.

During this period I also making some very good business and personal connections that I will tell you about later. They applied to me, and may very well apply to you also.

As we all need to understand, life has the ups and downs and although we had far more than our share of downs...all at one time it seemed, some very good things were happening both business wise and personally.

My confidence in myself and skills were solid but I knew that I had to be prepared for anything that may be coming our way, as we couldn't afford to lose the ground we had gained.

We received an unexpected blow when my mother -in -law who my wife had been taking care of suddenly dropped dead. Literally, just standing in her living room fell to the ground and died.

That was a tough one for me but it was just brutal on my wife. Remember, the outlined issues I have spoken of. Any one of those alone is enough to really crush someone. She had to deal with multiple catastrophes all at once and now, her mom was gone.

Losing a parent is tough enough and I was very concerned for her, as even though she hid it well, I knew she was nowhere recovered from what had happened to us.

In the movie Rocky Balboa, Rocky gives one of the all time great motivational speeches to his son. Part of his speech said this.

*"Life ain't all sunshine and rainbows, it's a mean and nasty place and I don't care how tough you are, it will beat you to your knees and keep you there permanently if you let it. You, me, or nobody is going to hit as hard as life. But it ain't about how hard you hit, it's about how hard you can get hit and keep moving forward: How much you can take and keep moving forward! That's how winning is done!"*

We had been living that statement and we were getting good at taking the hits. Maybe too good because about 45 days after my wife's mom passed I got a call from my Attorney.

*"Jim, I don't have good news. The Attorney General's Office is going to petition the Court to re-open your Bankruptcy. They are claiming you committed fraud"*

My reaction this time to the hit was different. I felt no fear, only resolve. I was VERY well aware of the game that was being played and there was no way I was going to lose. My Attorney was not concerned either as he knew the truth.

Unfortunately, the Court allowed the bankruptcy to be re-opened as they always give the benefit of the doubt the A.G's office. This move set my wife and I back again as everything needed to be put on hold and we were being denied the right to move on with our lives. The Judge however, being that a bankruptcy is Federal and I passed with flying colors, warned the A.G. that she better have something.

Her first move was to lie. She claimed she did not know I was in bankruptcy and therefore could not oppose it. That's odd, because both my attorney and I had e-mails from her claiming she knew. This not only showed her true colors but true character also.

I will admit that even though I had no concern over any of this, I was getting pretty pissed that a Government employee, working with tax payer money can work unen-cumbered with no fear of repercussions making me spend thousands of dollars on bullshit all the while abusing a system meant to protect not harm someone.

The Court date arrives as did she with three other Attor-neys and she presented... NOTHING! Her PROOF, which she claimed she had, did not exist. She asked for and was granted MORE time but harshly warned by the Judge that this was it. She was given 10 days to put up or shut up.

On day 9, she contacted my Attorney saying she was going to withdrawal the motion. She knew ALL ALONG she had NOTHING and knew the Judge would come down hard on her.

My Attorney and I decided we would not let her withdrawal and insisted we go to court so she could face the Judge. To say the Judge was angry would be an understatement. She admonished this Attorney and the A.G.'s office quite forcefully.

On our part, we asked for something called Sanctions. That means the State would have to pay my legal bills. The Judge threw the case out but we were not granted our sanctions. This was very rewarding as for the past three years we had beaten her at every turn and it seemed that this would be the final nail in the coffin.

My Attorney also let me know of some interesting findings that he had heard from other Attorneys. It seemed the A.G.'s office, in an effort to shine a positive light on the office, being that the Attorney General herself was under criminal indictment, was pulling out all the stops to try and nail anyone and anything that could help with the P.R.

I and who knows how many others were victims of a corrupt system the operated not for justice but for political gain.

My heart goes out to all those who may not have chose to fight as I did and were ruined.

One of my clients called me recently and said "Jim. Great news! We got a letter from the FBI saying any investigation into you is closed." Again, that was good to hear but I knew it was going to be the final outcome.

Unfortunately, the Deputy A.G. has not taken kindly to losing at every turn and is continuing her attacks on me. She has unlimited taxpayer funds in which to attack me and with the election coming up, she will be getting a new boss. It is imperative for her to make it look like she did something big in order to keep her job.

As far as how I feel about their latest attack? I have zero worries. After 5 years of just sitting back and being the "good guy" and "taking the hits" it now comes time to fight back. In situations like this you just cannot sit back and let yourself be abused. You need to courage to stand up for your convictions and fight no matter how big the odds may seem. Sometimes it may actually smarter just to roll over if the math works. But if it doesn't, keep your dignity and fight.

Evil hates the light, and sometimes exposing them to their own tactics is just what it takes to put the ball in your court. You DO have a First amendment right to free speech so don't let them silence you.

I only included this story so you can see what can and does happen to everyday people at the hands of unscrupulous Government officials.

It is ALL about money and political gain my friends and if you are an entrepreneur or business owner and you make over $150,000 a year…YOU ARE A TARGET! You need to believe me on this. You need to be VERY careful on a number of fronts.

CHAPTER **10**

---

# My Pain – Your Gain

If you have read this far, I am sure you may be shaking you head right now wondering how I survived.

Or, maybe you found some answers that you may have been looking for. If nothing else, I hope you see how adversity CAN be overcome when you apply the right strategies. And now for the fun part. I am going to tell you how I did it and more importantly for you, how you can use the very same strategies and thought process I used. This is NOT theory and can apply to both business and personal situations.

Before I list what strategies I employed it's important to understand that the most powerful weapon I had was FAITH. I don't know what your religious preference is or if you even have one but without the FAITH that this was happening for a good reason, I may have not made it. I also found strength when I should have been running on empty. It came from somewhere. I personally believe that someone is looking out for my family and me.

All the years of charitable work, the hundreds of thousands of dollars given to the needy, the acts of giving away debt free homes to returning veterans, working in soup kitchens and on and on all seemed to join together in some type of cosmic force that protected and strengthened me when I needed it the most. Yes, I believe that my deeds of the past bring me protection and, very soon, victory.

You also have a guardian angel...don't take it for granted.

Now, onto the strategies that worked for me and will work for you...

**1. Accurate Thinking.** This is something I feel is the most overlooked ingredient needed for success in both personal and business lives.

You MUST be able to access your situation for what it is, nothing more, and nothing less. This may be painful but it is a must. If you do NOT know where you are, how can you get to where you want to go?

I also understand that this can be difficult especially if you are facing a crisis and you are being crushed by fear and uncertainty. That being said, the fear you create in your head almost NEVER materializes. We always make things out worse than they really are.

The same applies on the other side of the coin. If you are doing well, do not think you are bullet proof. I did, and I got shot...with a bazooka.

Always be aware of where you REALLY are.

**2. Be Fit.** Fitness and health unfortunately take a backseat in many people's lives. I am not to get into the importance of everyday health right here but when in times of crisis however, you attention to your health must move to the front of the line.

This may sound odd when you are just trying to keep you head above water but I can assure you that without being in good physical condition....bad things WILL happen.

Stress is one of the top killers in our Country and we get plenty of it even when things are going well. When things are bumpy, we need to be able to balance out the toxicity with good health. PLEASE, do not take this lightly.

**3. Fundamentals.** The late great Jim Rohn once said,

*"There are no new fundamentals"*

Truer words were never spoken. When in times of crisis we tend to panic and start reaching for anything we can get our hands on in search for answers. The truth however lies in the fundamentals.

When I was forced to start over with nothing but my wits, I fell back on what brought me to the dance. I didn't look for some "new" magic formula. I went to what had always worked. Our success can sometimes be our own worst enemy and can lead us to believe that we are "above" the basics or that we no longer need the things we "think" we know.

Here is the best advice I can give to you on this issue. Do yourself a BIG favor and Google, John Wooden's lessons on socks and shoes. I think you will understand.

**4. Get better information.** If I had to point to the one thing that was the key to my successes it would be READ-ING. I literally have read hundreds of books on business and success and listened to thousands of hours of audio. When I became a "Big Star" I stopped.

I didn't think I needed it anymore.

As soon as I stopped, I started moving backwards.

When I took my big fall one of the first things I did was seek out GOOD information. As a society we are poisoned on a daily basis but negative programming both from the media and those around us.

You need to force feed yourself "GOOD, QUALITY" information. Here were and ARE still some of my choices for both good and bad times. For a complete list, check the back of this book.

- Mans Search For Meaning...Viktor Frankl
- Make It Big...Frank McKinney
- The Seasons of Life...Jim Rohn
- The Essential Wooden...John Wooden
- It's Not Over Until You Win...Les Brown
- Unfinished Business...Dan Kennedy
- Your Elephant's Under Threat – John Mulry
- How To Get Rich...Felix Dennis

**IMPORTANT NOTE:** None of these books are about making money. Even, How to Get Rich is about the RE-ALITY of Entrepreneurship.

Making money is simply a by-product of wise actions. The intangibles AND the fundamentals that you must have in your journey towards success can be found in the above books. There are many, many more but the above are books that didn't leave my side during my ordeal.

**5. Get around Better People, no matter where they are.**
As I look back on my wipeout, it is clear that my biggest downfall was surrounding myself with the wrong people. Making money was always easy for me but managing people was a different story. I tended to hire and spend time around people I "liked" as opposed to those that were "Qualified"

I am not bragging but I was at a level of success that very few attained. I was one of those evil 1% guys. But, I was surrounding myself with people that were not on my level and often times, taking advice from them.

PLEASE, do not take that as arrogance because this is VERY important. If you needed brain surgery to save your life, would you go to an auto mechanic? NO, of course not! So why then would you surround yourself with or take counsel from people "less qualified"?

I quickly discovered, albeit too late, that my weakness was just that.

As I began my road back, I sought out "NEW INFORMATION" from "NEW PEOPLE". When I was forced to start over the one thing I knew for sure was that I was VERY good at what I did.

I knew how to make money and I knew I could help people. I began to search for proven STARS that could see what I was looking to do and form a MUTUAL-LY beneficial relationship.

I turned to Bill Bartmann, a former Billionaire who went through something that makes my story look like a walk in the park.

Frank Mckinney, who to call World Class would be an understatement. Frank was and is more than a friend and mentor and always is there when I need his wisdom.

And then...directly from my arch enemy, the IN-TERNET...John Mulry from Galway Ire-land...YES...IRELAND!

Limitations are the killer of innovations and I see over and over again how people ONLY choose from those in their what I call "safe zone" Breaking news! The Internet has opened you up to WORLD WIDE possibilities and connections.

I understood that moving forward, I wanted to work with someone that "got" me and someone that could help communicate my message AND, add massive value in addition. It didn't matter how much I knew or how much I knew I could do unless the public knew. If you are a business owner...think about that.

I found John by an online search of VERY specific criteria I had laid out. He is a top-selling author, world-class mar-keter, AND, a genuinely good guy.

When I first talked to John, I was on guard as could be expected. I also happen to be a very good marketer and was very tuned in to BULLSHIT.

The story is too long to go into but the end result is that I am working with John and he is not only a trusted advisor, but also a friend. I hope someday you all get to meet him.

My point is that I am sitting in Scottsdale Arizona, do real estate deals in Akron Ohio and found my perfect marketing partner in Galway Ireland! LOOK BEYOND YOUR BOUNDARIES…because there are none!

**6. Focus on the NOW.** Living in yesterday is a big part of why many people are not as successful as they could or should be. You don't drive looking out your rearview mirror and you can't live your life like that either.

When going through a tough time you need to focus on the task at hand that is going to move you FORWARD. Even a small step can make a big difference. I believe a real smart guy once said, "an object in motion tends to stay in motion" Once you have your plan for how you are going to proceed, follow through on it no matter how slow the going may seem.

**7. Get Tough**. Here is some harsh reality. When you go through something like I did or you take some type of fall, do not be surprised if and when people leave you.

When I was hitting on all cylinders there were lots of people making lots of money off of me. I was the guy everyone wanted to be around because they made money from me. When I took the fall, almost ALL disappeared and I mean ALL. I can count on one hand those that were there for me.

This is tough because we tend to take it personally and many will be caught up in feeling sorry for themselves thinking people don't "like" them anymore. Listen, you need to toughen up and move on.

It would have been very easy for me to be upset with people that I took care of but were nowhere to be found when I needed it, but that is just human nature. Rarely does someone set out to "hurt" or "get" you. It is just the way it is.

LIFE IS NOT FAIR and you have it FAR better than most people in the world. No matter what happened, be grateful for what you have, stop feeling sorry for yourself and go kick some ass.

**8. Let It Go.** Multi-tasking is a myth and while you may have a few things running thru your brain at one time you cannot FOCUS on more than one thing at a time. When you are in a situation that requires maximum effort in order to pull yourself out of a hole, you have got to leave other thoughts behind. Using my story as an example, I had to REALLY buckle down and focus on what I needed to do to take care of my family.

I had so many things happening at once that is was easy to let my thoughts drift off to places they should not have been. When the Attorney General's Office was attacking me you better believe I wanted to fight back and get my pound of flesh. The problem with that was that all that did was make me angrier and clouded my thinking and judgment on things that were really important.

I know this sounds far easier than it really is but I can't tell you how important it is.  If you really feel the need to be pissed and plot payback, set aside time in your day for that specific tasks.  I'm not kidding.

If you need to do it, do it, but not while you are working on the important stuff.  If you have been wronged, let it go.  No need to waste your time on something beneath you.

# That Was Then. This is NOW.

Pretty hectic journey right? You can probably understand why I was so eager for Jim to share his story.

There are so many lessons to learn from it. Let's summarize this entire ordeal into a neat little package from where it began to where it is now.

**1. Lost his business.** Now, his business is back bigger and stronger than ever with a very powerful team around him (myself included). We specialize in working with entrepreneurs and business owners looking to make a quantum leap in their business. And if I do not mind saying so, we are loaded for bear!

**2. Nasty Bankruptcy.** Now, free and clear. Here is something you need to understand about a B.K.....it ain't fatal. You will be shocked to see how easily replaceable money really is.

**3. Dream home destroyed.** Now, Jim is living in one of the most exclusive and beautiful areas of the Country in a beautiful home that is LESS than what he was paying for his "dream home".

**4. Neighbors believed he was a criminal.** Now, very good and REAL people surround him. He didn't know it at the time but the neighborhood he was in was poison. The best thing that ever happened to be was getting out of that environment.

**5. His children were blackballed in the neighborhood.** Now, their lives could not be any better. His oldest has got a super boyfriend that she has been dating for 2 years...Jim jokes that he *"actually likes him"*. His daughter has also received a full scholarship to ASU...Arizona State University and is studying to be a Physician's Assistant.

His youngest daughter in a span of 18 months went from novice horseback rider to a Champion. Her room is filled with awards and she is one of the best in the Country at what she does. She IS living her dream

**6. Mother in law diagnosed with Alzheimer's.** Now, even though she has passed, it was an incredible blessing for Jim's wife to be able to be here for her mom and take care of her in her final years. You only get one shot at something like that and we were lucky we took it.

So there you have it. After Jim put his story down on paper we spoke at length about it and we both agreed that sharing his story is as much for his benefit as it is for yours.

Sometimes, putting your thoughts, feelings, frustrations and story down on paper can act as a veil being lifted so that light can shine through.

Now that we've shared Jim's story you might be thinking is that the end? This however is not the end.

No, it is just the beginning. For those that know Jim, I needed to let you know what happened and that he is back and there for you.

For those that don't know him...yet...I think this has been one heck of an introduction right?

# Time For the SIZZLE...

It's time to add some sizzle to your steak. And by steak I mean your business. You see that's what I believe a great marketing advisor or consultant or coach does.

They don't confuse you; they don't complicate things with flashy online 'magical' tactics that you neither understand now could care less about.

They take what you have already, make a couple of tweaks, add in some strategic sizzle and boom, you're off to the races acquiring more leads, converting them into customers and generating more profits.

Well that's my philosophy anyways and if I do say so myself I'm pretty darn good at it.

Chances are if you're reading this book you're an expert at what you do but the problem is JUST because you're good at what you do doesn't mean that customers are going to be queuing up at your door.

It would be nice if it was that way but sadly it's not.

So you have the steak, I'm going to add the sizzle.

Over the next few chapters we're going to walk you through some of these sizzling strategies in a way that has a key takeaway and steps you can take and start applying immediately.

CHAPTER **13** – JOHN MULRY

---

# Avoid These Unprofitable Mistakes...

When it comes to marketing and advertising, a lot of business owner's work mostly on disposable things of temporary value. This explains incidences of income but zero wealth.

People make this mistake in 4 different ways.

**Mistake #1:**

Investing lots of time in an employee that will stay a few years at best (who will more than likely willingly or unwillingly, knowingly or unknowingly rob you of your time, resources, money, and even potential business) while at the same time they under invest in systems or assets in their business.

**Mistake #2:**

They will also invest a lot of money in a pretty website and SEO engineered to draw visitors via organic search but once done and visible, it is easily and cheaply copy-catted which dilutes its value.

Not to mention that with this strategy which is one of the most popular (not a good thing btw) leaves you and your ability to get new customers at the mercy and whim of Google.

They can, have and will continue to dictate how and when you can get customers and at what cost and you're will-ingly let them when you focus on this kind of strategy.

While you're employing this strategy the big mistake is that you're under investing in complex, multi media, and multi step lead generation and selling in a vacuum sys-tems that are virtually impossible to copy.

Building a complex multi media multi step marketing SYSTEM isn't easy but when it's built, it's built and you can enjoy its fruits for years to come.

You could even bring all of your competitors into a room, walk them step by step how you built this system, show them the behind the scenes of how it would work, and they wouldn't dare copy you because well for one: they wouldn't be able and two: it's just *too much* work.

The thing is though, it he who has the system that wins.

It's he who can generate new leads and sales on demand that wins.

Which one will you be?

**Mistake #3:**

Another very costly mistake is developing and investing in products or offers that are quickly over and done with, intended for one time or short time use.

This is something I see nearly every day.

If you're focus is on the short term all the time you'll end up "begging in fall" as Jim Rohn eloquently used to say it.

He said: *"You have to get good at one of two things... planting in the spring or begging in the fall."*

Planting in the spring is the same as getting, either online or offline, clients. If you're not good at planting... getting clients, you'll surely be begging,... relying on price not value, and taking short cuts to make a sale, etc.

But planting in the spring is taking a long term approach and putting your time and focus on systems rather than quick fixes.

One and done is not a viable use of your time and re-sources.

**Mistake #4:**

The fourth mistake is creating a lot of advertising, marketing and sales copy built for one time use.

It has ZERO asset value.

It can produce income but there is no equity in it.

If you're constantly have to come up with new campaigns over and over and you don't have a system in place for attracting and converting leads you're constantly going to be struggling, constantly going to be chasing instead of attracting customers.

Hopefully that looking at those four mistakes you can spot the common theme in them.

The key is building marketing and advertising ASSETS that are a part of systems.

Think of this way.

In a sudden storm with little time to work with, it is a victory to get a tent up, or even a tarp tied between trees and a fire started.

But you certainly can't live there for years to come.

You want to build, not just do.

You need a house with a strong foundation that can survive the storms that will come and as you can see from Jim's story the storms will come.

Make sure you're not in a tent when it does.

The days of just being a good or even great merchant and prospering are pretty much over. It's a business model on life support. We must be more, be about more, mean more to our clientele than purveyors of goods and services.

Here's a quick barometer…

At least HALF of your investments of thought, time and money should be going to things that are NOT disposable and only of brief value.

It is fine to make income.

But owning assets is even better.

The strategic questions are:

What are you working on the most?

Are you building or doing?

**Writer Downer:**

You need to shift from once off promotions and fads to building marketing assets that work for you and your business.

---

# The Question You MUST Answer to Succeed

Any business owner can confirm, there are plenty of unknowns when it comes to being an entrepreneur.

- Should I have employees?
- Who's my target customer?
- How do I generate leads?
- What kind of website do I need?
- How much should I charge?
- How will I position myself?

But before you go too far down any of <u>those</u> paths, you need to ask yourself this critical question…

*What business am I really in?*

Here's the thing, as much as you think it is, it's not about the stuff you bottle, brew, make, produce, create, offer or sell.

Those are obviously important because you do need something to sell but...

The business you're REALLY in is...

## MARKETING

Most business owners view themselves as 'doers' of what they do... with the task of getting people to pay them to do it a necessary evil.

The 'doers' of things do those things and get around to marketing if there's 'time left over.'

How many times have you said to yourself?

- I'll get *that* marketing campaign done when I have time.
- I don't have time to market my business because I'm too busy working in the business.

This definition of who you are and what your business REALLY is has enormous impact on how you allocate your time and energy.

The business owner who focuses on marketing sees the acquisition, retention and value of maximization of customers as their primary role...

With the actual <u>doing</u> of the of the service the necessary evil.

Often "doers" will say they're no good at marketing or selling. Or that they don't like it or want to do it.

If you've said this in the past then you're boxing yourself in to forever being a "worker bee" rather than a "Queen Bee," and to forever working harder rather than smarter.

In preparation for this book I did some research on the life of worker bees.

Worker bees, sole purpose in their lives is to work for the queen bee. That's all.

As a business owner, you don't ALWAYS have to be a worker bee.

**You can and should be the QUEEN BEE.**

After all, when you're running a business, it's you that's taking all the risks, it's you putting your neck on the line, it's you that's providing jobs and stimulating the economy, and since it's you taking on all that, don't you deserve the spoils that come with that?

Well of course you do...

Technical skills related to the delivery of a quality product or service is important – but those are not nearly as important as the ability to market those same products or services.

By focusing MORE on becoming an accomplished Marketer, you massively increase your potential for wealth and success.

Marketers are much more valuable and highly paid than "doers". This is very difficult for "doers" to accept but the bottom line is that if you want to increase your personal earning power in the business you're REALLY in, the answer is always to focus on becoming better at MARKETING and not at Making.

Too many business-people are product obsessed, or technology obsessed, and completely misunderstand what it is that their customers are really buying.

Even businesses selling tangible products are really selling INTANGIBLES.

Marketing your business boils down to the considerations of your customers. What THEY want and how THEY view what it is you sell.

1. People are easily stimulated to optimism and generally prefer feeling optimistic to pessimistic, given the opportunity to feel so.
2. People long to make things better. They may not be willing to work very hard at it, but the urge is there, always bubbling beneath the surface.
3. People join churches, multi-level companies, start businesses, move to new towns, enter new relationships, go on diets, etc. all based on the hope that doing these things will make them richer, happier, thinner, and healthier.

In short, people invest in **<u>HOPE</u>** time after time, pretty much regardless of how prior similar investments have worked out.

When you take the time to understand these things about what people want, desire, and need, then you can incorporate them into how you market your business.

Now, I'll be going deep into the HOW of this in later chapters but for now consider what Charles Revlon had to say about this:

*"In the factories we make perfume, but in the stores we sell hope."*

Revlon demonstrated that he dearly understood this and some key truths about the people he chose to become his customers.

The "professional marketer" masters the skills of direct marketing without being limited to any one product category or media.

**When:**

- The perfume maker becomes a marketer of fragrance.

- The online business owner becomes a marketer of online products/services.

- The coffee shop owner becomes a marketer of fine coffee and food.

- The financial planner becomes a marketer of financial planning.

...he or she takes a quantum leap up in income potential. No matter what business or industry you're in... you're REALLY in the marketing and advertising business.

And because this is the business that you're REALLY in you better figure it out...

And how do you do this?

Well, that's what I'm going to walk you through now!

# The 3 Factors Limiting Your Marketing Success

Listen, I completely understand if this big bad crazy world of marketing and advertising is completely bamboozling, confusing and never endingly frustrating.

**I get it, I genuinely do.**

The reason you're so bamboozled by it all, isn't because you're stupid or because you're behind the times or anything, the reason is actually because there's so many "gurus" and experts out there who make it way more complicated than it needs to be...

They do this on purpose, to keep you confused, because it's to their benefit not yours. They make their business off of your confusion.

We much prefer to educate you on HOW to market successfully, without any of the hype or confusion because when you succeed as a result, you'll become a champion of what we have to offer.

On top of that, the dizzying array of new media's and new technologies coming out can cause more confusion but the thing is, whether or not you do or don't succeed has nothing to do with all of those new media's and new technologies but three simple to understand factors.

What are those factors?

I want you to think of your marketing as a triangle.

## Triangle of Marketing Success/Failure Factors

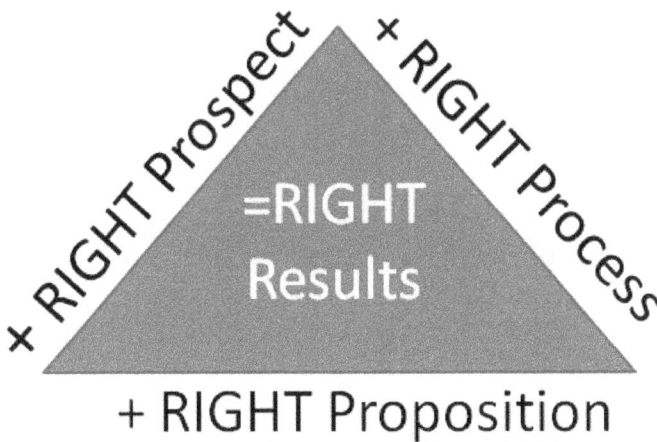

+ RIGHT Prospect

+ RIGHT Process

=RIGHT Results

+ RIGHT Proposition

If something's not working, it's because at least one of those three factors is incompatible with the others.

Every success is the result of getting all three right.

Every failure is from misfires in one or more of the three.

Let's go through each one in detail.

## #1 Right Prospects:

**The right prospect has to have**:
- A **need or desire** you cater to,
- **Care about getting an answer** to that need or desire, and
- **Be able to pay** your price for that answer.

It's as simple as that. Don't waste your time or resources pitching to any other kind of prospect.

**You need a means of...**

1. Finding and/or attracting only those prospects and
2. Driving away all others, as early, quickly and cheaply as possible.

Also, please note, when it comes to targeting and when it comes to choosing your market, the easy decision but often times the most costly is trying to please everyone, trying to attract EVERYONE and ANYONE.

*This is BAD FOR BUSINESS...*

Trying to please everyone, trying to attract everyone is the same as attracting no-one.

This may seem counter-intuitive but trust me you need to be very clear and up-front about who you <u>are for</u> and who you <u>aren't for.</u>

Yes, this means you'll be repelling some people but this is a good thing.

When you're clear about who you don't want to do business with it becomes very clear to YOUR TARGET AUDIENCE who you are for, thus they are more open to engaging with you, your marketing collateral and are more opening to putting their hands up and telling you they are interested in doing business with you.

## #2 Right Proposition:

Like I mentioned you need to be crystal clear about whom you are for and who you are NOT for.

By doing this, you'll be able to put together a very FOCUSED message or proposition to that market.

This is where the magic happens.

Why?

Well, because plain, vanilla, ordinary, uninteresting or incomplete propositions are out of sync with the "New Economy Consumer".

**What or who is the "New Economy Consumer"?**

The New Economy Consumer is essentially every consumer in every market today…

These days, with the rise of globalization, the rise of the digital selling and the lowering of barriers to entry in almost every industry has led to one problem for businesses...

The power is in the hands of the consumer...

They are literally spoiled for choice in almost every category and when they hold all the power when it comes to choice.

This is VERY BAD NEWS for generalists and those businesses whose marketing, messaging and propositions are BORING.

But similarly, this is GOOD NEWS for you when your message, your proposition is tightly focused and is very specific.

Your proposition has to fit your prospect to a tee.

**Essentially, your marketing needs:**

- A terrific proposition
- A strong "Unique Selling Proposition"
- A strong "Unique Value Proposition"
- An irresistible offer
- A reassuring guarantee

Here's an example...

A proposition that is all about saving money is very motivating to some, but not likely to inspire an affluent consumer to go there versus another place, nor sooner than need warrants; they don't buy on price.

The affluent are more likely motivated by a <u>proposition</u> of **exclusivity or perks or unique** *experience* such as a special closed-to-public evening at the restaurant with an entertainer, wine-tasting, etc.

## #3 Right Process

Once you have the right prospect and the right proposition the final piece of the puzzle id the process.

The Right Prospect + The Right Proposition and The Right Process is the exact same as the core MMM (message, market and media) triangle that every success and failure in marketing is based upon.

The Right Prospect = Your Market
The Right Proposition = Your Message
The Right Process = Your Media

Media is THE LAST step of the whole process yet, nowadays more so than ever it's where people start first.

When I ask you about marketing and advertising, you immediately start thinking about things like:

- Your website
- Your business cards
- Your brochure
- Your catalog
- Your Facebook
- Your Twitter
- SEO

- Email
- Direct Mail
- Newspapers
- Radio
- Etc.

The thing is though, these are not marketing, these are methods of DELIVERING your message to your target market.

If you have a shoddy message delivered to your target market – it won't work.

If you have the right message delivered to the wrong market it won't work.

**This is why the RIGHT PROSPECT and the RIGHT PROPOSITION is so important.**

Once you have that, the last part of the triangle is EASY.

You just deliver your message to your market in every way possible, but there are some things you want to be aware of:

- You need to match your process to your prospect.
- And you want to match your process to your proposition.

Ideally, you match your Process to your Prospect. For example, when selling by direct-mail, it's almost always better to be selling to people who buy by direct-mail (vs. a list of TV infomercial buyers).

You also match Process to Proposition - does it need to include diagnosis? Demonstration?

Also, when it comes to delivering your message, pay attention to a method of media they are used to, open to but also pay attention to methods of media that you can reach them on but that are not that competitive.

For example, online methods of communication are all the rage these days but methods of media like Direct Mail. TV and Radio are STILL valid methods of media (when done right) and with something like Direct Mail you can take advantage of the fact that not many people use it today.

How many personal letters do you get each day/week? One? None?

Similarly...

How many emails do you get on a daily/weekly basis?

Hundreds? Thousands?

How many times have you put a direct mail letter, postcard, or coupon onto your fridge for later use versus how many times have you printed off an email to keep later?

You've probably never printed out an email unless it was a boarding card for a flight right?

Don't dismiss traditional media, and certainly don't dismiss it as a method that "doesn't" work anymore... if it didn't work in the past, chances are that's because you had either:

- The wrong message
- You were targeting the wrong market

Now, I'm not some old curmudgeon who is anti new technologies and new methods. I use the most advanced, latest cutting edge methods to deliver messages to markets for myself for the Wolf Pack and for our clients but we DON'T LIMIT ourselves to one method.

We use as many as it takes.

You have to remember that different people have different buying preferences and buying styles. Some people won't read but will watch video or listen to an audio.

Some people won't dare buy anything online (or don't know how, or can't) and similarly some won't buy over the phone.

In fact, there a lot more people who won't buy online that you think, and funnily enough a large majority of these are affluent and super affluent.

So if you rely solely on selling online, how much profit are you losing out on each and every month?

In closing off this chapter, it comes down to this...

If you're looking for ways to boost sales, there are only three places to look:

- The Right Prospect (Market)
- The Right Proposition (Message)
- The Right Process (Media)

For me this is the sexy part of marketing but hey, I'm weird, I understand if YOU don't think this is as sexy as marketing funnels, as campaigns, as shocknawe packages, as automation and all that super sexy stuff but all of that stuff doesn't work UNLESS you have those three pieces in place.

Implementing this isn't easy. It can be tough figuring this out, and while we can accelerate this for you with our done-for-you programs and systems the reality is that this will take work.

The most successful business owners do what at least 80% to 99% of business owners WON'T do.

Not can't do.

WON'T do.

# The Simple System To Making Sales Without Being 'Salesy'...

Now that you understand the prospect, proposition, process trifecta – we can start digging into to how to go about implementing it.

And how to actually do it in a way that's not frightening, intimidating or confusing, but in a way that leverages what you ALREADY KNOW and packages it in a way that attracts your target audience like an unsuspecting moth to a flame...

And best if all, we're going to do it without being salesy...

**Here's the big secret...**

You may want to grab a highlighter or heck put this in a big BOLD type at say 100pt font size and stick somewhere in your office, practice or home where you'll see it every single day...

People will come to you faster and stay longer to learn something (of value to them) then they will ever come to you to be sold to.

That's the secret right there... those 27 words hold the key...re-read that sentence again so it sinks in.
When it comes to the application of the marketing strategies I've walked you through the bottom line is this...

To get the best results possible, instead of advertising your business, advertise SOMETHING OF VALUE to your target audience...

When you do this you cross the threshold and become an information marketer...

And no matter what you're business is – being an information marketer is a VERY good marketer to be...

**Why? Well for starters here are three reasons:**

1. Materials perceived as information are better received and given more attention than materials perceived as just advertising.
2. Salespeople have sales literature. Trusted advisors have information.
3. Advertising free or nearly free, useful information is a low-threshold offer.

Typical advertising and marketing that doesn't offer anything of value but merely advertises the business is only attracting a very small percentage of people in your target audience. High threshold offers like a visit with a salesman a test drive or dental exam are useful but solely using them means you're missing out on and deterring a large proportion of people who would otherwise be interested in what you have to offer.

**Here's what I mean.**

This is something the late great Chet Holmes popularized years ago but sadly it's been forgotten with the rise of the fancy and distracting new gadgets, gizmos and shiny objects in online marketing and media.

The problem with 95% of ads and marketing materials out is that they are trying to sell from the page.

**Marketing and advertising is like dating...**

To get the best results when it comes to dating you cannot just walk up to a complete stranger you've never met before in a bar, nightclub, coffee shop gathering, event or wherever and say

"Hey, I think we should get married, have three kids, two dogs and a cat." – At best you'll get laughed at, at worst you'll get a slap or a drink thrown in your face...

It's the exact same scenario in business ... why oh why do we think its okay to go out and try and get married on the first date?

That's what selling from the page is...

Have a look at ads online, in magazines, newspapers and on the radio, the majority are trying to jump straight to marriage and kids...

Sure you can pick up some customers this way but when you sell from the page generally what's happening is you're attracting customers who shop based on price and you're only attracting now buyers...

At any given moment no matter what it is your business is selling out of your target audience there is only 3% who are actively looking for what it is you sell...

Only 3%... that's it.

And this doesn't mean 3% of whoever sees your ad – it means 3% of your target market who see your ad.

That's a big distinction.

After the 3% of people actively looking to buy next up comes 7% of people who are open to what it is you have to sell. These are people who aren't in buying mode but are on the lookout.

Even combining those together is only 10% of your potential market.

**What about the other 90%? Well:**

- 30% of these are open to it but are NOT AC-TIVELY thinking about it…
- 30% THINK they're not interested and finally
- 30% are definitely not interested…

When you understand this dynamic everything changes… these figures aren't made up… these are based on empirical evidence from more than 200 industries and on average these are the figures…

And the best way to start tapping into the other 90% or at least 60% f it is by using some informational offers that are either free or low cost.

**What are some examples of informational offers?**

1. Useful information that educates your target audience on how to make better decisions as it relates to your product/service industry.

   For example – a free or low cost book (like this one).

2. Useful information on HOW TO BUY

This could (or more like should) be a book or DVD, CD on things your potential customers must know before they do business with you (or anyone).

**For example:**

11 Things You Must Know About Health Clinics, Weight Loss Clinics and Weight Loss Specialists BEFORE You Purchase.

If your target audience is people looking to lose weight – what's going to work better – advertising your business or advertising a FREE booklet, video, DVD or CD on the 11 things they must know before buying.

This is so simple is genius.

Here's a template you can use no matter your business or your industry.

**\_\_\_\_ Things You Must Know About _____, _____ and _____ Before You Purchase.**

Here are some examples:

- The 7 things every homeowner should know about plumbing repair, boiler servicing and radiator damage before ever hiring a plumber.

- The 9 things parents should know about crèches, daycare facilities and Montessori schools before they ever enroll their kids in them.

- The 5 things every doctor, health clinic owner or cosmetic surgeon should know before they ever spend money on advertising and marketing (this is one of our own by the way).

As you can see these are not complicated.

Other variations of this are:

- **Everything you ever wanted to know about before buying _____ but were afraid to ask.**

- **The Consumer's Guide to _____ and _____**

- **The buyers Guide to _____**

This type of informational offer that shoes people how to buy is so valuable to them and to you it makes you the only logical choice when it comes to making a decision.

Like I said it's so simple its genius.

You don't have to be a marketing guru to do this.

You're simply taking the knowledge you already have and you're packaging it up in a way that your target market will want.

*That's what information marketing is all about.*

And best of all, you do the work once and you can use it again and again and again.

I get very excited about this stuff.

I know what you're thinking and you probably have some questions right?

## How many points do I use – 11, 7, 10, or what?

Use as many as you want to use, I'd say stick with a minimum of 5 but usually 7, 9, 11 or 13 are good starting points.

## What should I talk about in the points?

Talk about things your prospects should know in order to make better decisions. This is easy, there is so much information that you take for granted that your prospects have no clue about.

Simply educate them while combining that educational material with future pacing – i.e. – getting them to imagine what their life will be like after achieving their desired result as it relates to your product or service.

## How long should it be?

It should be as long as it needs to be. No longer nor shorter. Warning there's a lot of idiots out there peddling that copy be it in a video on website in a letter or anywhere should only be a certain length and that any longer and it won't be read.

Pure hogwash and those peddling that nonsense are uneducated fools.

Harsh? Possibly but the fact of the matter is that the difference between success and failure with your copy does not come down to length it comes down to how interested they are in it and how engaging it is.

For example, you're reading this book, if people didn't read long copy then all books would only be one page and all movies a couple of minutes.

Yet movies are 2-3 hours or more and books have a couple of hundred pages on average.

The length needs to be as long as it needs to be.

I was once asked this question and I eloquently answered it in a way that's worth repeating and definitely worth remembering:

*The best copy is neither long nor short. Neither better in print or in video neither spoken nor read. The best copy, the copy that evokes a DIRECT RESPONSE is as long as it needs to be... Not a word longer or shorter...*

**Should I include anything else?**

Yes, of course but you want to be strategic about what you include.

Here's a starter list of sections to include in your own strategic lead generation magnet:

- Table of Contents
- Your Story

- About Your Business (In terms of what you CAN do for them)
- The X Things They Need to Know
- Next Steps
- Offer Specific for Readers
- Testimonials
- Frequently Asked Questions
- Questions You Wish Your Prospects Would Ask
- Contact Information
- Re State Specific Offer for Readers

See, not in the slight bit complicated – and when you've this finished you've something that will generate leads for you night and day.

You can offer it on your website, hand out printed copies, have offers for it on your business cards, and create ads offering it in newspapers, magazines online on Facebook, Twitter etc.

**When people request it they telling you:**

1. They're in your target audience
2. They need and want a solution to a problem
3. They're ready to buy

Can you understand the power in this?

And best of all it's not rocket science – you could put this together in a few days.

Do the work once and profit from it again and again.

It will become your biggest marketing asset and will transform your business.

Full training on how to do this FAST is available at www.expertauthorityformula.com

Now if you don't want to create this yourself myself and Jim have programs where we'll work with you to create it, now this isn't cheap but we'll be working with you to create an irresistible lead generation tool for your business that when used it will bring in more leads and customers that will be worth many many multiples of the investment to get it created.

Reach out to us if you're interested.

By the way, this strategy as amazing and exciting as it is isn't new. As you'll see below in two examples from 1934 and 1918 – informational marketing has been around a long time – but don't disregard it for that reason, champion it for that reason.

There are also a couple of other types of informational offers that you can use to help facilitate sales also:

1. Information Offer used as FREEMIUM for buying. For example in 1934 Pulvex which sold flea powder used an n informational guide as a freemium or gift with purchase to boost sales.
2. And there's also information offers used as media for advertising. In 1918 there was a bride's cookbook that was chock full of useful information but

also had adverts from businesses that were target-ing married women.

Useful information packaged up in this manner will always be in demand from your target market – never forget that.

In closing off this chapter remember:

To generate more leads you can convert to customers, use VALUE BASED INFORMATIONAL offers.

The key word there is value. You need to strategically position your value based informational offer in front of your target audience and preferably have a closed gate be-tween them and the information.

And in order for them to get access they have to give you something in return – their contact details.

So you can follow up with them.

For full, free, in depth training on this process visit:

www.expertauthorityformula.com

## CHAPTER 17 - JOHN MULRY

# Putting Your Marketing System Together...

Now that you understand the fundamentals of the right way to market your business let's look at how this all fits together.

Again, I'm going to break everything down in a simple to understand and easy to implement fashion.

When it comes to marketing your business there are generally two pots you want to focus on:

1. Marketing to generate new leads, sales and customers.
2. Marketing to existing customers and clients to maximize average transaction size and transaction frequency.

The second pot can be just as important as the first because the process to get a customer is straight forward; the cost can be significant (depending on your niche, positioning and process).

Since this is the case, it's natural then that marketing to existing customers and creating ladder of ascension for which they can climb (each rung represents more of your products and/or services) makes complete logical and business sense.

This is a topic for again and is actually something we pay very close attention to with our private clients.

For here and now however I'm going to outline a simple system you can use for pot number 1: Marketing to generate new leads, sales and customers.

It comes down to three areas:

- **Attraction**
- **Conversion**
- **Automation**

Within those three areas there are three sub areas to focus on.

Like I said, I like to keep things simple. No need to overcomplicate everything. Get this down FIRST then maybe add in the fancy stuff later on to see if we can improve upon things.

**Attraction:**

- Create a low barrier to entry offer you target market can't refuse.

This is the information offer I talked about at length earlier. Create this or get us to create it for you but bottom line you're going to need a strategic lead generation magnet that ATTRACTS your target audience.

- Advertise this valuable offer to your target audience.

Once you have created this MAGNET you need to switch your advertising focus from advertising just your business, your products and services and start advertising this instead. I've already discussed why this is so powerful; if you need to be reminded, read the previous chapters.

- Use multiple methods of media.

Don't just rely on one method of media. Use multiple media online like Facebook Advertising, PPC, Your website, SEO, banners etc.

Don't neglect offline either have posters created offering the informational offer and details how they can request it.

For example they may be able to request it by:

1. Calling your number
2. Texting their contact details
3. Visiting a specific landing page on your website
4. Calling in store.

Use whichever one suits your business best but whatever you do make sure that in exchange for this offer you get contact details (full contact details if possible).

**Conversion:**

Once you've attracted the lead that's only the first step.

No point in getting a lead if you don't do anything with them right?

- Have a SPECIFIC follow up process in place.

The reality is that not everyone (and likely only a small number) will convert immediately. You must have a specific follow up process in place that does the following things:

1. Delivers what you offered them.
2. Introduces you and indoctrinates them.
3. Offers them a solution to their problem (your product/service)
4. Continues to add value to them.
5. Continues to communicate with them.

- Qualify your most IDEAL clients.

You must also qualify your leads so you can focus on those who are the hottest versus those who are not quite ready right now.

And bear in mind, there is nothing wrong with lukewarm or cold leads. With the right follow up process in place those leads will either mature or turn into referrals further down the line.

## How do you qualify your leads?

The easiest way to qualify your leads is by a quick survey asking them specific buying questions or making an offer to them early and sees which ones go for it.

- Use the diagnostic 'non salesy' method of closing (W.Y.L.H.W.T.)

When it comes to actually closing the sale – people get so hung up on it.

1. They are afraid to ask for the sale
2. They are afraid the prospect will say no.
3. They think they're not salesmen.

The thing is though, when you have setup your marketing and advertising the way I've shown you here, the sale becomes easy.

No you're not going to close everyone, you never will, but you needn't be frightened by it or intimidated by the thought of making the sale either.

And if you're thinking that you're not a salesman or that you weren't born a salesman then relax because and I think it was first Zig Ziglar that said, no one is born a salesman, there's never announcements that a new baby salesman was born, sales is a skill that be learned.

Better yet, sales are something that can be facilitated and made easier by the right marketing.

When you setup your marketing system the way I'm describing to you, your sales 'pitch' is just six words...

W.Y.L.H.W.T

**Would you like help with that?**

That's it. And if you done your job like I previously outlined, than more often than not, the answer is going to be yes.

Sure there are other strategies and tactics you could use but you won't need to. You'll be generating so many leads that are qualified and who will WANT to do business with you won't need to use any of that extra stuff. You can, but that's just the icing on an already delicious 'full of yummy sales' cake.

**Automation:**

Now you might be thinking:

Isn't this an awful lot of work?

And you're right it is, and if you deterred from hard work, we certainly won't be working together.

The beauty of all of this however, is that once this machine is built the bulk of it will work for you, not the other way around.

- Use systems that automate everyday process.

You're going to use marketing automation to take care of the attraction and conversion process for you. And your follow up process will be nearly all 100% automated too.

I say nearly because I don't believe in true 'set and forget' programs. A personal touch of some kind is always needed and will always improve results dramatically.

- Do the work once but benefit from it again and again.

Automation leads to autonomy. When you use automation you get the benefit from having systems that repeat process for you that can be very time consuming.

You can automate tasks such as sending out your informational guide, automate the capturing of and qualification of prospects, as well as even automate the whole selling process.

This is the BIG benefit of building a marketing system that is an ASSET – it works for you.

- Build a system that WORKS for you on autopilot.

Yes, this hard work and I would be lying if I said it was going to be easy to set all of this up but once its set up it will be like an army of employee working for you 24/7 without all the headaches that comes with having employees.

Jim will cover these headaches and how to deal with them in an upcoming chapter but the bottom line is that marketing automation will lead to freedom in your business.

Imagine being able to automate the attraction and conversion or your leads and sales?

This isn't a pipedream; we'll show you exactly what is needed for this if you're interested. Reach out to us – we'll be happy to help.

In the next few chapters Jim is going to walk you through other sides of your business that are crucially important outside of your marketing.

I hope you're enjoying things thus far, oh and by the way, we are just getting started...

# It's All On You, Baby

This is not a strategy, per se. It is *the* ingredient to success. Yes, there really is one, and this is it:

*Work harder on yourself than you do at your job.*

—JIM ROHN

Despite his death, Jim Rohn not only continues to be one of my mentors, but he was a mentor to hundreds of thousands, if not millions, of entrepreneurs throughout the world. His best known student is Tony Robbins, the world-famous self-help guru.

Jim Rohn said that the problem with most people is they continue wishing for some*thing* to get better and hoping that will change his or her circumstances.

Many people are looking to change some*thing*, but that is not how it works. What needs to change is you. That's when everything else gets better.

When I first heard Jim Rohn's words all those years ago, it took a while for them to sink in. I really think it was so obvious that I missed it. I was a young entrepreneur, doing what I thought was my best but I was still struggling.

I kept wishing for things to change . . . on the outside.

I hoped for the real estate market to change. I hoped the people I was surrounding myself with would change. I was looking for everything to change, except me.

I believe it was Gandhi who said, "Be the change you wish to see in the world."

I probably heard *that* before too, but I never applied to me.

Eventually, it sunk in. And it really didn't take that long. What a simple, but powerful statement. "Work harder on yourself than you do at your job."

This is the secret: If *I* get better, then *everything* gets better.

I was not necessarily sure it was going to work, but I had nothing to lose. So I went to work...on ME. I became an information junkie. I bought every book I could find on business, real estate investment, marketing, and so on.

---

## Education and Personal Development

I enrolled in what Zig Ziglar called the "automobile university."

I did not get into my car without a personal development tape program ready to play as I drove. I listened to thousands of hours of motivational and business programs.

I received a world-class education in my car.

I bought biographies on all the great leaders. I learned from THEM what to do and what not to do.

Here is a news flash for you:

Any problem you may have in life and business has been experienced by someone else before you. You can find out how they solved that problem! That, to me, was unbelievable. Like most entrepreneurs, I thought I was on an island all alone.

No! It's all been done before, and the answers are just waiting for you to pick them up.

I also took the advice of one of my other truly great mentors, Charlie "TREMENDOUS" Jones, who said:

*You will be the same person five years from now as you are today except for the books you read and the people you meet.*

---

## Who Do You Spend Time With?

I had the book and audio thing down, but I was still lacking on the "people you meet" part.

What that means is, "Who are you hanging around with?" This can be a killer for you and your business unless you deal with it *now.*

When I started my career as a real estate investor, I surrounded myself with people that were, to be kind, not up to par. On a personal level, all my friends were broke and complaining about everyone and everything which, unbeknownst to me, had a very bad effect on my attitude.

No one in my inner circle took personal responsibility.

Looking back, that's why I was stuck for so long.

When I read deeper into Charlie's quote, I realized that he didn't just mean people, he meant better people. Yes, in my business life, I had people who were so-called "experts" in their field. Realtors, contractors, finance people, etc., but they were not *really* experts, they were just in the business.

I began to seek out the *BEST* that I could find.

Once I did this, I noticed a rapid and dramatic jump in my income. Next, I began to withdraw from many of my friends of the time. I was growing and they were not. They needed to go. This may be difficult for you, but here is the reality.

Not everybody makes it.

Some need to be left behind.

This may sound harsh, but that is the way it is. If you have an inner circle that does not *completely* support you and are striving for the best in their own lives, you need distance yourself from them.

This was not an overnight process. There were still bumps in the road, but as each day passed, I grew better equipped to handle the realities of entrepreneurship.

My priority and your priority, was and *must* be **WORKING ON YOU**.

This is not an option.

You *must* make your main focal point YOU!

- **YOU getting better**
- **YOU getting around better people**
- **YOU getting better information**

These are the keys to the kingdom.

This is why great franchises can be so good for some.

They provide all the ammunition you need to become successful. Information. Product. Team. Backup. Everything.

You can walk into any McDonalds, anywhere in the world, and an eighteen-year-old kid can be running the show. Why? Well it's not because they have the market cornered on smart eighteen-year-old kids. It's because they have made it fool-proof by providing the necessary information, systems, tools, and people.

This simple concept changed my entire life.

If you look at my bio it looks pretty impressive. What makes it even more impressive is that I barely made it out of high school! I was **not** a book smart individual. I would have never made it if it had not been for that piece of advice. I can say with full confidence, that advice creates miracles.

---

## Brain vs. Brawn

There is more to it than just feeding your head. You need to take care of the body. Oh, I can hear the groans now. Pay close attention to me on this. The mind and the body go together.

If one is lacking, all is lacking.

You cannot operate a business at its highest level if you are not physically fit. I'm not talking about being a body builder or world-class athlete, but fit. And fit as you can get for your age unless you have some *serious* health issues that would prevent that.

I have worked out my entire life and I am in better shape than many who are half my age. Just a fact. I work at it. Do I like going to the gym? No, I hate it!

I do, however, like the results.

And the results also register in financial form. The biggest crisis this country is facing is not the economy, but health care. Almost 50% of Americans are considered obese.

Have you ever heard the term, "survival of the fittest"? Well, it's true. Not only will you last longer than the competition, you will attract more business.

You must make yourself attractive to the marketplace in all areas. Product, service, and appearance. Deny it all you want, but people gravitate to attractive people. I didn't say it's fair, but it is what it is.

Refer to my opinion on "fair."

To win in today's business climate, today's *very competitive* climate, you must be on your game at all levels. You have no choice but to take an active role in being as physically fit as possible. And yes, you have the time.

You need 30-45 minutes a day of vigorous exercise, along with a sensible eating plan to keep yourself at the top of your game. I suggest a regimen of weight training, assuming you have no physical ailments, along with twenty minutes of daily cardio.

And I don't mean walking at a snail's pace on a tread-mill. I mean *vigorous*, "break a sweat, work your body" effort.

You have been given the greatest machine ever created. Care for it. If you do, you will be rewarded. If you don't, you will pay the price. If you need help, hire a personal trainer.

And what about that eating plan I mentioned? Sooooo much misinformation out there, where do you start? You're in luck. I happen to have forgotten more about nutrition than most so-called experts know.

Hey, it ain't bragging if it's true.

Almost 70% of your fitness level and physical appearance will be derived from the eating plan and 30% from working out. Most people think the opposite.

They think they can eat as much as they want as long as they work out. Unless you're burning 5,000 calories a day, you need to watch what type and how much fuel goes into the machine. And even if you are burning big calories, you still need the right fuel.

Here is the easiest and best plan you will ever find. If it doesn't walk, fly, swim or grow out of the ground, don't eat it.

I just saved you all the trouble of going out and wasting money on useless diet books and programs. The above-mentioned plan is how we are genetically programmed.

All this nonsense with processed foods, bread, sugars, was not meant for us and I think the result is pretty obvious. To compound the problem, we not only eat the wrong things, we *overeat* the wrong things. Add that to the stress of being a business owner *and* not exercising, you can see how disaster could be fast approaching.

If you really want to take a serious interest in your health, which you must, check out www.Bevnutcom. This is the website of Beverly International the Countries leading producer of supplements that WORK.

---

## Booze

And last but not least . . . it's got to be five o'clock somewhere. Look, this is the tough one for lots of people.

The booze.

I get it.

The life of an entrepreneur, for all its great rewards, does come with stress. Lots of it. I also know that sometimes a good shot of whiskey can go a long way. I know that some time at the bar after a hard day can provide a measure of relief.

I also know that sometimes . . . the party never ends.

I have been blessed with some type of freak genetics or maybe Irish blood that allowed me to drink . . . a *lot* and still be productive.

Or so I thought.

It was only after I stopped drinking, that I realized how unproductive I was. Yes, I was functioning, but when I look back on what I could have done had I not been drinking, it's pretty sad. Not to mention the fact that excessive drinking will ruin any fitness plan you may have.

I am not, nor have I ever have been, an alcoholic.

I am one of those people who can say, that's it, I'm done. I still enjoy a good martin but for the most part I have seriously backed off.

If you can, I suggest you consider doing the same. It's not the end of the world. You may shock yourself at how productive and less stressed you become. If you can't quit . . . get some help. There is no shame in asking for help in this matter. We all have demons that we need to keep locked away. And I mean we **ALL** have them.

Even the ultra-wealthy and super-successful.

Deep down, we are all the same. No one better, no one worse. If this is your demon, keep it in the cage. I promise that having a clear head will have a positive effect on more than just your bottom line.

The lesson in this chapter is exactly what we started with. Make YOU getting better a priority.

"Work harder on yourself, than you do at your job."

If you don't read, start.

Now!

If you do read . . . Continue and add to it.

Buy and listen to tape/CD/MP3 programs; podcasts, personal development, business, marketing, and any other subject that will help you grow. We provide you with a list of "must haves" at the end of the book.

Network and reach out to those who can help you get to the next level and eliminate, or at least distance yourself, from those who holding you down. Find people who are **better** than you at *everything!* You will be pleasantly surprised how the most successful people are always willing to help or pass on some good advice.

Take a serious interest in your health. And I mean serious. You must become attractive to the marketplace. Mentally, physically, and with your products and service.

When you follow this plan of self-improvement in your life, magic happens. You will wonder what happened as things that were once so difficult now come so easily. This is no smoke and mirrors, this **WORKS**. It is timeless wisdom that can turn your life and business around. I know. It did for me.

---

## Momentum

And now the *warning*.

I also know what happens when you stop.

You see, I did everything that I have recommended to you. And guess what? I became a big success, I made *LOTS* of money.

As a matter of fact . . . obscene amounts of money.

I was the big dog and I was too smart for my own good.

I thought I knew it all.

I was so smart I decided that I no longer needed to follow the principles that got me to the dance. I stopped reading, listening to audio programs, stopped working out or at least half-assed my way through my workouts, and it all . . . began . . . to crumble.

It took me almost a year-and-a-half to figure out what was happening. I was looking everywhere to point the blame except for where it belonged.

With me!

What snapped me out of it? Wouldn't you know it was the same thing that made me successful? I remembered a quote by my friend, the great Les Brown and here is what it said:

## WRITE THIS DOWN AND KEEP IT WITH YOU:

*Life is a constant battle for territory. The minute you stop fighting for what you want, what you don't want, automatically takes its place.*

That was the answer I had been looking for.
- I had stopped fighting.
- I had stopped reaching.
- I had stopped growing.

Thankfully, I was able to recognize what was happening and course correct. I assure you that I will never make that mistake again.  I say, without hesitation, that I am now better in every way than I have ever been.

There is no tomorrow.  Only today.

You need to focus on being the very best you can be and you need to do it *now*.

Either cut down or eliminate all forms of distraction in terms of outside messaging.  This means the internet, social media, the news, and so on.  This is nothing more than mass brainwashing and if you think it does not have an effect on you, you are dead wrong.

Focus **_only_** on **_you_** getting **_better_**.

If what you have around you or going into your head or your body is not adding, then it is subtracting.

Get rid of it.

When you get better, everything gets better.

Trust me.

You will get many valuable lessons from this book, but this is the one that I hope you take to heart.  **You** are the most valuable asset you have. Don't blow it.

# One is the Loneliest Number

When Three Dog Night recorded that song I wonder if they knew what great business advice it would be. One "anything" in business can put you in a position you do not want to be in.

Andrew Carnegie once said:

*Put all your eggs in one basket, and watch that basket very closely.*

Now far be it from me to question the wisdom of someone like Andrew Carnegie, but I'm going to. Rich, does not always mean right.

Why? Because, as they say, "Shit happens."

You get bored, things break, people leave, trends change and on and on.

When change occurs, which it always does, you need to have a fallback position. As a matter of fact, oftentimes you may find that the fallback position takes the place of the primary position.

So, the word of the day is...DIVERSIFY.

Just look for examples at Apple, Trump, Richard Branson, and many other very successful individuals. They branch out into as many things as they can, knowing that some of these ventures will fail. They don't go into it "knowing" it is going to fail, but they understand that in business, sometimes things just don't work out. They also are taking advantage of the leverage multiple income streams operated simultaneously can bring.

Listen, it is very important for you to understand who you really are. You are an entrepreneur. You are not a coffee shop owner or a landscaper or a fitness trainer, YOU ARE AN ENTREPRENEUR.

Entrepreneurs go where the money is. Get it? As some of my clients down south say, "Yer a money finder and getter." Yup, I am, and so are you.

So what you need to do in addition to working on and growing your primary gig is to actively begin to scout out more and more opportunities to make more baskets.

I can hear some of you now disagreeing with me by thinking that you "are" what you "do." No, you are not. Ray Crock was a milkshake maker salesman. How did he go from that to owning the biggest restaurant chain in the world? He knew he wasn't "just" a milkshake maker salesman.

He was an entrepreneur.

If you are not in a constant state of evolution, you are edging closer to a state of extinction.

So what kind of basket do you look for? Well, that depends, as there are more opportunities out there than you can count. I personally like investment real estate.

Let me make my case here. Some of you may be thinking I am promoting investment real estate because of my past and current history with it. I think that it is very important for you to understand however, that I got into the investment real estate biz, not because I liked houses. I got into it because I liked MONEY.

Many moons ago when I finally came to the realization that the "traditional" path to making money was not working, I set out to find something that would. Frankly, I didn't care what I did as long as it would supply me with the money I needed to live the lifestyle I was looking for.

So I went out to look for my basket. It didn't take me long to make a very important discovery...RICH PEOPLE HAD REAL ESTATE.

As a matter of fact it was Andrew Carnegie himself who said:

## "MORE MILLIONAIRES HAVE BEEN CREATED THROUGH REAL ESTATE THAN ANY OTHER ENDEAVOR."

That was all I needed to hear. Remember, I didn't know anything about it, didn't really care about it, and I didn't have the necessary skills. None of that mattered.

I am not going to go into my entire back story in this chapter but what I will say is that within 45 days, I had made more money than I had made in working six months at my job. The best part is that it was passive income, meaning that I did not have to physically work for it.

Here are some of the reasons you can and should consider making investment real estate one of your baskets.

1. It is a tangible asset. Meaning you can see it, touch it. It's really there and not just your money floating out in the ether.

2. It is an active market. Unless everyone plans on moving out into the street, you will always have an active market and it will never go out of style.

3. OPM. In case you don't know what that is, it's Other People's Money. Yes, you really can get into this biz all by using someone else's money.

4. Passive Income. This is the big one. Investment real estate can run with minimal involvement from you. This gives you the huge advantage of spending your time doing the things you really want to do.

5. Low Risk. There is nothing you can get into that is a no risk venture and I mean nothing. Walking across the street has risk. The question is, "What degree of risk?" In the investment world, risk and reward ratio goes hand in hand. This means if you want to get a high return on an investment, you are looking at high risk. If you want maximum safety, you will be looking at a very low return. Real estate offers the opportunity for a very high return with a very low risk. It is an entirely different animal in the investment world.

6. Opportunity for Profit. This was the big draw for me in the beginning. I wanted to make LOTS of money and make it fast. In this business, averaging

$25,000 - $50,000 on a flip is not a freak occurrence, it is the norm. Add to that the fact that you are doing it with other people's money, time, and talent, and you have the greatest thing since sliced bread.

7. Flexibility. This is what makes it such a good basket. As I said earlier, this business can truly run with very little of your involvement. Whatever your primary baby is may require a significant amount of your time. By adding real estate, you add the potential for huge additional income with very little time involvement.

Those are the big seven. Obviously there are many more opportunities out there other than investment real estate, but I think it is one of the best, if not *the* best. Remember our golden rule. GO WHERE THE MONEY IS.

And the money, lots of it, is in investment real estate.

So go out and build some more baskets.

Don't be fooled into thinking you are not in the extinction line. Many, many others much bigger than you have ignored this rule with disastrous results.

Just ask the record companies.

# Employees...

No cute title for this chapter. "One word will suffice," he said as he wrote the word, teeth clenched.

I found this chapter difficult to write and it will probably be difficult for many of you to read:

- Many of you will not want to hear what I have to say because you are in denial.
- Many will read and nod in agreement with what I am saying and do nothing.
- Some of you, the smart ones, will underline, re-read, and *ACT* on what I am saying.

Your choice.

Before I go any further I will concede that there are exceptions to every rule. Obviously, there are great employees out there and some of them may be with you. I get that.

However, from a *sheer numbers* point of view, the odds are stacked against you. You are far more likely to have average or below average employees. As for thinking you have well above average and exceptional employees?

Well, as the old saying goes, "Even a blind pig roots up an ear of corn every once and a while."

Sometimes you get lucky, but not too often.

In fact, very, *very* rarely.

Much of how the odds lay will be determined by how carefully you bring someone into your business. Hire employees with your *eyes wide open* so you are not blindsided. For those of you new to the employee thing . . . this will help you plan. For those of you already in the water, this will help you course-correct.

I do have a bit of experience in this subject as I have had as many as thirty employees and as few as one. The number of employees isn't what counts. It's how you manage them.

If you can't manage one, you can't manage thirty.

The reason I said this is difficult for me to write is because I don't have much to say about "it". Frankly, I could sum up the entire chapter in one paragraph. That however will probably not sink in as you may assume that the brevity equates to importance.

Nothing could be further from the truth.

As a matter of fact, I could fill an entire book on this subject. In my coaching programs, I do go into this subject in *MUCH* greater detail.

For the purpose of this book though, I am going to keep it brief, but not too brief.

---

**Necessary Evil**

These two words fit quite well.

Unfortunately, most people cannot go it alone in business without some type of help. There are some small businesses where you can pull it off and a number of franchises that lend themselves to this option. Outsourcing, too, minimizes the need for full-time employees for some types of business.

In my opinion, the fewer employees you need, the better. But sometimes you do need a few.

Let me begin with my philosophy on employees. Now, some of you liberal, touchy feely types may be offended by this so be warned.

## *THE ONE AND ONLY PURPOSE OF AN EMPLOYEE IS TO PUT MORE MONEY IN MY POCKET AND MAKE MY LIFE EASIER!*

Sound harsh?

Hey, sometimes the truth hurts.

How did I arrive at this "philosophy"? I was born and raised in Homestead, Pennsylvania, a suburb ten miles outside of Pittsburgh.

My father worked in the steel mills his entire life and instilled in me what I feel to be a very strong work ethic. At one point, I even considered getting a job in the mills when I graduated high school. That is until my dad taught me a lesson I will never forget. As a matter of fact, I can remember his words like it was yesterday.

When I told him I wanted to follow in his footsteps, he said, "You need to find something else to do with your life. The mills will not be there by the time you graduate high school. You cannot pay someone $8.00 an hour to sleep all night. The union demands for more pay for less work will be the end of it all."
Well, he was right. The union demands did help put an end to the steel mills.

The mentality was that if the company made more money, the employees should make more money whether it was deserved or not. Not only did they feel that way, they abused the process. My dad told me about guys working the overnight shift who would *SLEEP* all night and then brag about it. $8.00 an hour was a lot of money back in 1979, especially when you're paying for someone to sleep.

My point is this. The entire country has been over-whelmed with an entitlement mentality of, "Give me more, give me more. I don't want to have to earn it, just give it to me."

Fortunately, or unfortunately, this is how I view em-ployees. My experiences only serve to emphasize my dad's observations. I've had a lot of employees over the years and without exception, I repeat, *without exception* at some point or another they all developed that entitle-ment mentality.

I can hear some of you saying, "Yeah Jim, I can see your point, but I have some very good people working for me." Well, I'm sure you do. I did too. Or at least I thought I did. I thought I had people who were *so* loyal they would be with me forever and follow me to hell and back.

Guess what, they didn't and they don't.

The basic instinct of the human being is survival.

155

*Their* survival, not yours.

If it comes down to you or them, trust me, they are not going to worry about you or your family.

It is absolutely critical for you to remember this.

If you are looking for loyalty, get a dog, not an employee.

## THE ONE AND ONLY PURPOSE OF AN EMPLOYEE IS TO PUT MORE MONEY IN MY POCKET AND MAKE MY LIFE EASIER!

Yeah, I said it again.

On purpose.

Your reasons may be different, and they never cease to amaze me. If I listed all the stupid reasons people hire employees, this would be a very long chapter. But the above mantra should guide you.

If you appreciate the seriousness of my statement, let's move on to *who* fills the role you have available and *what* they will be doing for you.

Whether you need a single key person or you need fifty employees will depend on your business. In my experience, many business owners bring in more employees than necessary, others don't bring on enough.

The key to success is to know exactly how many people you need in order to obtain maximum productivity and maximum profits.

---

**Hot Tip**

Just because you need something done doesn't mean you have to hire employees. Many needs can be met by outsourcing. A restaurant can't outsource the cooks, servers, etc. But a small gift shop owner who needs a website doesn't need to hire a full-time web designer.

Make sense?

So, assuming that you **DO** need employees . . . how do we manage and deal with these kids?

First, you make it very, very clear why they are there and what is expected of them. This is the biggest reason employers have problems with their employees. It is super important to let them know up front, the philosophy of the company. You need to bring in someone who "gets it." Most, however, will hire someone who will bring more misery than anything else. Why?

157

You didn't explain the rules!

Compare this to real estate investment. The biggest reason landlords have trouble with tenants is because 99.9% of the time, they didn't explain the rules. When the rules aren't explained the tenant makes his own rules, i.e. not paying the rent, prostitution ring, drug dealing, etc.

Employees are no different.

They may not run drugs or be the local pimp, but they *will* play when the cat is away . . . You must clearly outline the duties and responsibilities of any and all employees.   If you do not, why would you be surprised if they did not do what you want them to do?

I mean really?  **WHY** would you be shocked?

Yet so many business owners want to point the finger at rotten employees when in fact, it is the business owner who is the problem.   That's not to say the employee wasn't a bad choice initially, but to make an employee a good one is *your* responsibility.

---

**The Plan**

Outline very clear and detailed responsibilities that can be measured and managed. **Write** them down. If you can't measure it, you can't manage it. Your employees can't perform well when they don't know what is expected.

Once expectations are clear, you must manage the process, which doesn't mean hovering over their shoulder every minute. If you have to do that, you hired the wrong person.

With this kind of structure you can track progress and measure results.

Here is a list of *my* deal-killers in terms of employees:

---

## Tardiness

This to me, is a "do not pass go, you are done" card. I totally understand that there are times when being late cannot be helped. But, those times are very few and far between.

Maybe I am a bit anal, but my philosophy is that if you are not fifteen minutes early, you are late. When people are consistently late, that shows a **BIG** lack of respect for **YOU**. In effect, their tardiness says that their time is much more important than yours.
Sorry. You're done!

I strongly recommend that you make this very clear to any potential employees, and that there is no quarter given. If you choose to let someone into your business with this habit and attitude, I absolutely guarantee that they will burn you at some point.

When you have a tardy employee, immediately sit down with them and get it handled. Even if you need them for whatever reason, let them know their tardiness will no longer be tolerated. No other explanations needed.
*You* own the business.

If this tardy employee is one you simply haven't got the guts to fire...then put on your big boy or big girl pants and **FIRE** them. Once you do, let everyone know *why* you fired them and that you will no longer tolerate lateness.

"But Jim, they might get mad at me."

Whaaa. Whaaa. Whaaa. Toughen up. I am going to repeat this over and over and over until you get it.

This is *your* business.
This is *your* livelihood.
This is *your* paycheck.
Forget the touchy-feely crap and run your business like a business. If you want to do charity work, go to your local church.

## Misuse of Time

When you are paying someone to perform a task that means they need to be performing the task. Silly me, expecting someone to do what I am paying them to do. But I *DO* expect someone to do what I am paying them to do.

I suggest you be silly too. I'd bet that you would be horrified if I installed some hidden cameras in your workplace and monitored what your employees are doing with *YOUR* time.

If I were to do that I could tell you they are surfing the web, making personal phone calls, chit chatting with other employees, sleeping, and any number of things that do not pertain to the job you hired them for.

And you're *paying* them to do these things.

So how do you deal with this? Well, the first way is to prevent it in the first place. Just as with being late, this needs to be dealt with up front or if you already have employees in place, immediately after you read this.

I recommend a zero tolerance policy in dealing with these issues. I know that sounds harsh and maybe it is. As a result of my past experience, when I was overly lenient on these issues, I found myself making excuses for them.

I didn't want to be the "bad boss" because I wanted everyone to like me.

Being the nice boss didn't work for me and it won't work for you.

---

## Promises, Promises

I had employees that I swore up and down would never ever do anything to hurt me. I would bend over backwards for them and I was sure my kindness and loyalty would be rewarded.

It wasn't.

Of the two of the people I put at the top of that list, one embezzled a couple hundred thousand dollars from me and helped put me out of business and the other quit out of the blue and went to work for a competitor she had consistently bad-mouthed.

On another occasion, the real estate brokerage where I was co-owner hired a property manager that I had a funny feeling about. Nice guy, almost too nice . . . a real schmoozer. I had a bad vibe about him from the start. I couldn't put my finger on it, but I knew something wasn't right.

However, I was not in charge of this individual and my partner, who was the broker of record, assured me that it was my imagination.

One day, I was contacted by one of *my* clients asking me about potential deals that were being sent to them. I had no idea what he was talking about until I saw the e-mail.

This property manager was using **MY** database of customers to sell **HIS** real estate deals on the side!

As you can probably imagine, I was just a little bit ticked off.

My partner however, though it was an honest mistake and that he was a valuable employee. Honest mistake? Soliciting my database without my permission? No, not an honest mistake. Backdoor theft is more like it.

I made the mistake of letting my partner talk me out of firing him and just letting him off with a warning.

The thing is where there is smoke there is fire and this kid would strike again.

Sure enough, not long after, we began receiving calls from clients asking about their rent payments. It seems they had not been receiving them. When my partner at the time *finally* agreed to confront him about this, the kid gave another song and dance.

Then he quit.

We found thousands of dollars in rent checks in his desk that had not been deposited. He had been spending his days *not* out at client properties but out looking for his own properties all the while being paid a salary by us.

He left quite a mess for us to clean up. The real fault, however, belonged to my partner and me.

I knew something was wrong. My gut told me from the start that something wasn't right. We should have taken a closer look at the guy in the beginning. We definitely should have fired the guy after the client solicitation incident.

I violated my own rule. I let my partner talk me out of listening to my gut.

---

## Are You Listening to Your Gut?

I'd put up a significant wager that some of you reading this have employees right now who you have a bad "gut feeling" about.

And you're trying to convince yourself that "things will work out."

Please, that's no different than when you were a kid and you pulled the covers over your head telling yourself there is no monster.

When you were a kid, you were right.

This time, the monster is real and ignoring it is a *huge* mistake.

There is a reason the phrase "hire slow, fire fast," has been around for so long. You alone are responsible for your employee policy; what you will tolerate and what you will not tolerate.

My tolerance level is zero. Unless it is a really small issue, you don't get a second chance with me.

---

## Hiring Employees

Let's back up for a minute and assume that you don't have any employees, and you have determined that you absolutely have the need.

How do you hire? All right . . . we're getting to it.

165

## BUT FIRST . . . A "YOU BETTER LISTEN" WARNING

Below, we'll be discussing how to find and hire the right people, but before the actual hiring takes place do your *due diligence.*

I learned in the real estate investment world that a lot of things can creep up and bite you in the wallet. In that world, the number one problem is landlord-tenant issues. Horror stories abound about bad tenants.

But the blame doesn't lie with the tenant.

The blame is squarely at the feet of the landlord . . . more specifically, the landlord who did *not* do appropriate diligence. The tenant lied and you didn't check.

It's a harsh reality, gang. *People LIE!*

And if people lie to become a tenant . . . they will lie to become an employee.

Potential employees will lie about everything: past work history, current work history, personal history, education history and so on. They will lie to suit their needs. It's all the rage now to put in bogus resumes to potential employers in order to get a position.

I knew a guy who bullshitted his way through his interviews to get a six figure job. His prior background? He was a *very* good used car salesman. He employed those same tactics to get his new job. It took them six months to catch on, but the point is he got hired and paid for those six months.

Don't think it can't happen to you.

---

## How to Do Due Diligence

No matter what someone's resume says, no matter how nice they are, no matter how good looking they are . . . check them out completely.

You think I'm kidding? I'm not.

Find out:
- Do they drink?
- Take drugs?
- Have a criminal record?
- Been fired in the past?
- Been dishonorably discharged from the military?
- Are they a head case?
- Too meek, too hard?
- Are they willing to submit to drug testing?
- Can they provide proof of any stated education?

You get the point. You should identify the traits you are looking for in an ideal employee and work from there.

I suggest that you do an extensive background check for employment history and criminal background as well.

I hope that we are in agreement that it is **always** best to nip a potential problem in the bud. Do not ignore your instincts or give in to your needs. Keep your eyes open and as Ronald Regan said, "Trust, but verify."

Nuff said…back to hiring.

---

### Who NOT to Hire

## *Do not hire family and or friends.*

Hey, it's only my opinion. But the odds are that at some point, something will go wrong, and possibly very wrong. If you want to preserve the relationship, it is best not even to put yourself in the position.

Do you want to have to fire your brother-in-law? Your sister? Your uncle? Some relationships are worth preserving, so don't put them at risk.

*Do not hire someone just because they're "looking for a job."*

Too many business owners do this. They hire anyone for anything.

Can you believe it?

Instead, you need to hire the very *best* person for the job who is willing to accept what you're willing to pay them. And you might be interested to know that you may have to pay a little more to get the *best*. But it's worth it.

The people who are the *best* at something don't come cheap.

Remember, "buy cheap, buy twice," or in this case, "hire cheap, hire twice."

It's not good enough to hire someone who will just "get by" in a position you need filled. Verify that they have the necessary skills to do their job well.

Pretend you're looking for a date.
Not just any date, you're looking for **THE** date. The one who will turn heads, make your friends jealous, and your mom proud.

You want quality, and it's out there.

---

**Forrest Gump**

What are the intangibles you are looking for? Hopefully you've identified the skill set needed but this is different. What in addition to that skill set would make this a great hire.

Not good hire . . . a **great** one.

*Forrest Gump* is one of my favorite movies. Maybe one of yours too. If so, you will remember the scene when he told his beloved Jenny, "I'm not a smart man." Sorry Forrest, but I disagree. You *were* a smart man. A *very* smart man. Why?

### *BECAUSE YOU FOLLOWED INSTRUCTIONS!!!!!*

Yes, Forrest followed instructions all throughout the movie and he ended out on top every time.

He . . . paid . . . attention.

That's who we want, Forrest Gump. And if you can't hire Forrest, hire someone like Forrest who can and will *follow instructions*.

This is where it all begins gang.

So let's throw out some bait.

Wherever you should choose to advertise, I would suggest that you place an ad with clear yet potentially confusing instructions.

Confusing instructions?

I know. This may sound a bit odd, but it goes to how well someone can follow instructions. Most people tend to gloss over instructions and figure that they've "got it" with a quick glance.

Unfortunately, in the business world, that "quick glance" can end up costing you a lot of money.

Here is a cool example of following or not following instructions. As a matter of fact, it was such a powerful lesson for me, I have never forgotten it.

I was in sixth grade, yes, that long ago, and we were given a pop quiz. Don't you just love those? Anyway, the quiz was twenty questions long, multiple choice, and a twenty minute time limit to complete.

When the quiz was handed out, the teacher *emphasized* that we were to read instructions before beginning.

At the top of the quiz were the words, "Read Instructions Before Beginning."

I wasn't prepared for the pop quiz.

Everyone knew they were under a time limit.

As I worked through the problems, I was surprised. It was a pretty easy quiz. For me, this was good news. I was not the sharpest tool in the shed and I needed all the good grades I could get.

I blew through that quiz, feeling pretty confident that I'd aced it. Then I got to the last question.

Huh?

It wasn't a question. It was a statement. It said, "If you have reached this final paragraph, you have failed the quiz. The instructions told you to **NOT** answer any questions." Yikes!

A big fat "F" all because I was in a rush, and I assumed that instructions on a pop quiz could not possibly be important.

I have never forgotten that lesson.

As I said earlier, in the business world, this can be disastrous. Imagine placing a $20,000 media buy with specific instructions as to when the spot times should be only to find out the sales rep "didn't pay attention." That could blow your entire campaign. Not only do your employees need to be able to follow very specific instructions, you need to be sure that *anyone* you are dealing with can follow them.

I kind of got ahead of myself there but I wanted to be clear that when hiring someone, they need to be able to "do your bidding" so be sure to test before you buy.

---

## Free Thinking (within reason)

So, what else are we looking for? Personally, I like free thinkers, but not too free. What I mean is that I do not want a mindless drone, of which there seems to plenty of these days. I want someone with a little bit of creativity.

Here is an example of how this can fit with any employee.

I had an accountant for years who was just a great guy. He was very good and kept me out of trouble. Eventually however, my business had gotten so big and was bringing in so much money that he actually came to me and said that he felt it was time to step aside as things may be getting too big for him.

I appreciated his honesty and we parted on good terms.

I then went out a hired a highly referred CPA who specialized in small business owners. At our first meeting he asked for a copy of my past few years tax returns so he could review them. I wasn't quite sure why he wanted to do that but I didn't question him.

About a week later I received a call from him and he asked me if I would like him to re-do the returns. I asked why, and he informed me that my accountant did a good job . . . a good job for the IRS! He said that the returns were done in an *ultra*-conservative manner and that my previous accountant did me no favors at all by performing in that manner.

I was shocked.

My accountant, who probably thought he was looking out for me was actually hurting me by not pushing the envelope and taking advantage of things that could *legally* be taken advantage of. He was not acting in a creative manner at all. Instead of reaching out a bit and getting a little creative, he chose to stay exactly in the box they set out for him. The result was thousands of dollars on over-payment of taxes that I should not have paid.

Well, let's just say that we fixed that problem. My point is this, something even as mundane as accounting can use some creativity.

---

## Appearances can be Deceiving

This is also one of the reasons I am not big on appearances of people I hire. Unless they are in a direct position of dealing with the public in a manner that "acceptable" appearance is necessary, I don't really care.

I don't care if you have piercings, tattoos, long hair, shaved head, etc. Obviously, hygiene is important but you get what I am saying. I am not concerned with publicly accepted "norms."

Many of the geeks and freaks out there are the most creative people and make some of the best employees.

Do not under any circumstances hire based just on appearance unless you are running a modeling agency or some other type of business that requires, "the look".

By the way, all you guys out there that hire some hot chick because . . . she's hot? I will say the odds are probably very high that will cost you in one way or another. Think with your wallet not your "you know what." Same goes for you ladies out there although you are clearly not as shallow as my male counterparts.

---

**Communication over Looks . . . Every Time**

Even though I am not concerned about their appearance, I am concerned with communication skills. I am a stickler for this in most cases. Again, depending on the need you have, this may not be that big of a deal. If your employee need is a floor sweeper, you probably will not need a thespian.

On the other hand, in many if not most cases, we will be looking for someone fairly literate. This is especially important with anyone who will be doing any type of phone work. People tend to equate IQ level with speech patterns and accents. Think about it, and be honest, if you hear a Southern accent, I'll bet you automatically deduct about thirty IQ points.

Right?

Obviously I am not saying to exclude anyone with an accent. As a matter of fact, rightly or wrongly, people are often prejudiced. If you hear an English accent on the other end of the phone, many people equate that with sophistication and class. On the other hand, if you hear an Indian accent, often our first response is anger because another American job has been outsourced.

Your phone people are generally the first point of contact, so be sure whoever is in that role is a fit. This is not hard, gang. We are looking for pleasant, well spoken, well-informed people who are **NOT** pushovers.

In many cases this person will be your gatekeeper.

Another very big plus would be sales skills.

What? You say your phone people aren't in sales?

176

You're wrong.

*Everyone* is in sales. Some not as obvious as others, but sales nonetheless.

These criteria should be followed for **ALL** your phone people or anyone dealing with the public. Think about this for a minute. We are all in the "people" business. And in this business, you need to be able to navigate in such a manner that you end up with your desired result.

Here is an example.

One of my businesses was the real estate investment world. In dealing with rental properties one of the avenues I always took was subsidized housing or to use a more familiar term, Section 8 housing.

When dealing in the subsidized housing world, you need to deal with caseworkers and inspectors who are government employees. They hate their jobs and they are miserable most of the time. They get landlords and tenants calling them all day long, yelling at them.

What you need to know is that *they* hold all the cards.

So, what was my approach? Simple, I killed them with kindness. I laid it on heavy. I told them how much I admired that they could do such a tough job and how pleased I was with their service. I would send thank you cards and sometimes even ordered pizzas for the office I was dealing with.

Guess what? I got whatever I wanted. Why is this important?

Well, if you call down there like many landlords and mouth off about your inspection being late or complaining about anything else in the process, they will put their foot on your neck so fast you won't know what hit you.

It won't be obvious, but it will happen.

An inspection that could take place in a few days is now delayed for a few weeks. This means *no rent* for however long this takes. Do you see where I am going with this?

This means *money out of your pocket.*

Sometimes we need to play the game, gang.

This is what I mean when talking about how your employees should be dealing with the public. We always want to make the public happy. When they are happy, they spend money.

When they are not happy, they don't.

Having employees who communicate well with the public is *not* a luxury for your business, it is a necessity. I don't care if you own a little coffee shop or run a manufacturing plant. All people want to know that they are understood and appreciated.

The communication between you and your employees, and your employees and the public needs to be at the top of the list.

So, hire right.

---

## Measure and Manage

Isn't it funny how the things you that you hate doing the most are sometimes the most important? Yup, get over it.

Measuring what your employees do and more importantly, "managing" them is something most business owners dislike. They either avoid it or they do it half-assed.

That is a very expensive way to operate.

It doesn't matter if you feel you have made the best hire possible, you still must track what your employees are doing as well as "directing" them as you see fit. Many business owners simply hire someone, give a brief description as to what is expected, and then turn them loose. It is somewhat amusing at how stunned these employers are when said employee goes sideways on them.

So let's start with measuring.

As I stated earlier, communication is supremely important in the success of any business. In this case, I refer to the communication between you and your employees. In order to measure their performance, you must know what the end result should be and how long it will take.

Here is a set of clear instructions you could give to a secretary, customer service rep, etc.

"I want you to do ten-minute courtesy calls to these twenty clients, and supply me with a brief report. I need it to be done by noon."

That was very clear, right? Yes, it was. Clear, to the point, with specific instructions that you can manage.

How? Simple math.

If the workday starts at 8:00 a.m. and lunch break is noon, you have four hours. I clearly instructed said employee to do *ten-minute* courtesy calls. These are not "Tell me your entire experience with us" calls, these are quick, "Hey how are you, we love you and wanted to make sure you love us," type calls.

180

20 clients x 10 min are 200 minutes. 200 minutes equals 3.3 hrs. Start at 8 am. You can do the math.

This is simple stuff. The task may not even take ten minutes per call. At least 30% of the people you will not reach and have to leave voice mails. 20% will be quick calls no more than five minutes.

The remaining may take the full ten minutes. This gives *plenty* of time to complete the assigned task.

"But Jim, you want them to give a report, too."

Yes, but I want the Cliffs Notes version, not *War and Peace*.

Here is my reasoning behind this. As I demonstrated with the basic math, this is a task that takes under four hours. However, what *many* business owners do is this:

"I need you get call these twenty clients and make sure everything is OK."

See any problem there? I hope so.

If you didn't, let's just say things are a bit open ended. You can bet your sweet booty that many employees will make a full day out of this task if they are not given a *deadline.*

It's called ***work***, for a reason. If you forgot the only reason to have employees, go back a few pages and refresh your memory. When you are paying someone, with ***your*** hard-earned money to perform a task in an efficient and timely manner, you are a fool if you do not enforce it.

Now, let's say they have that task completed in two hours, then what?

As I stated earlier, this is why it is so important ***not*** to hire non-thinking drones. This is why you need someone with some initiative.

This is also, once again, where communication comes in. A good line of communication will have this laid out before the task is begun.

"Oh great and wonderful boss, once I complete this task, what I can do is jump right on _____ (insert any project here), what do you think"?

See what I mean? Leave nothing open-ended. This sounds like a "self-starting" employee, but if you don't give specific instructions you might find yourself with an employee who spent the last seven hours just waiting for you to tell them what to do, or worse, they'll get involved in something you don't want them working on.

Listen, if you feel like tossing out your hard-earned money to a bunch of do-nothings, be my guest. I can tell you from firsthand experience that many employees spend their days, and your money, surfing the web, making personal phone calls, etc.

The day ends and not only has nothing been accomplished, the dummy business owner doesn't even *know* nothing has been accomplished. He is too busy putting out fires to even worry about it until it is too late.

## *ALL EMPLOYEES MUST BE GIVEN CLEAR, DETAILED, AND MEASURABLE TASKS*

Your job as a business owner is to know the daily tasks you want to have accomplished, how long they should take, and the results you are looking for. If you cannot do that, you need to hire someone that can do it for you. I completely understand that most entrepreneurs and not good managers. I get it.

However, that does not excuse the need for management should your business have employees.

That, my friend, is *still* your job.

# Big Brother is Watching

Another way to monitor what your employees are doing is by video surveillance and monitoring of computer systems.

WHAT??!! I can hear you now. "That's not fair. What do you mean track what they are doing? And watch them?"

Perhaps you are confused as to what type of enterprise you are running? Is it a "business" or is it a "charity"?

I am not going to waste any more time convincing you. I am just going to tell you what to do and let you decide.

Ignore me at your own risk.

Step one is to get your hands on any one of a number of services or software that will allow you to view in real time, exactly what your employee is doing at any given moment, from any location. You will also be able to view past visiting places they may have wandered onto. You can literally track, minute by minute.

Video surveillance is another tracking method that thankfully seems to be more prevalent these days.

Listen, you ARE being watched. Like it or not.

For God's sake they were able to catch the punks who did the Boston bombing within a few days just by video feeds from department stores. Forget whether you feel it is right or wrong.

It just IS!

I also strongly endorse it for watching employees.

As much as you may not want to believe it, sometimes people go bad. Workplace theft is ridiculously high in this country. If you happen to be the owner of that business, guess who pays the freight?

If you are thinking that these measures will be detrimental to your employee's attitude I beg to differ.

When are you on your best behavior?

When someone is watching.

If you have employees who really want to keep their job, and they know they are being watched and tracked, it is probably a safe bet that they will perform.

---

## Environment and Pay

Speaking of your employees being happy or unhappy let's discuss workplace environment and pay structure.

Workplace environment. Listen, much of this is common sense. You obviously want to "within reason" do things and or provide environment and circumstances that keep employees happy. Key phrase, "within reason."

A workplace is a workplace. I know that the current trend is to have these incredible facilities that cater to their every need, which in turn makes them a happy-happy, joy-joy employee who kicks ass and stays forever. It seems the hippie movement is still alive and well.

That looks good on paper, but I know that not to be the case.

I have two close friends who happen to work for a company that was recently voted the best work environment in the country. They beat out the legendary GOOGLE facility. I have been to this facility and I can tell you that it is truly a sight to see.

I mean it is a fantasyland with everything you could imagine from movie theaters, to coffee shops to restaurants to dry cleaners and on and on. I am not easily impressed but I can say that I was blown away. I have been to many of the top luxury resorts in the world and none of them had anything on this place.

I am not going to name the company as they're a multi-billion dollar "privately" held company and I don't want to get sued for what I am about to say.

They provide an unbelievable fantasyland for employees. But as with most fantasies, it doesn't last.

Word is that most employees last only three years. I won't get into the reasons. The point is, the "feel good" work environment is not in any way shape or form a guarantee of employee productivity.

I am not advocating Spartan work conditions, but I also do not recommend going out of your way to create a workplace that will have your employees singing *Kumbaya* every day.

The basics are the obvious. Clean and safe. I also prefer an environment that stimulates some creativity but that is your call. Also, depending on your business, you can add to "clean and safe" as you feel needed. Again however, I have seen firsthand that workplace extravagance does not equal a positive outcome. It may help, but it is certainly not the be all end all.

## Proper Care and Feeding

Just a joke.

You see, I live in a zoo.

187

Not really, but close.

My daughter, Natalie, is the animal whisperer and she whispers to them to come to our house. Chickens, horses, dogs, gerbils, lizards, and spiders . . . you name it. Anyway, all animals should have proper care and feeding.

So should employees.

Feeding, they're on their own. Yes, that was a joke too. But care . . . that is a different issue. When I say care, I am talking about their compensation. Compensation that is fair. Not too much, not too little and with the potential for "earned rewards."

Emphasis on "earned."

We live in an entitlement society and I don't see any signs of that ever changing anytime soon. This has spilled over to many segments of society, including employees.

This all began with Andrew Carnegie and his workforce at U.S. Steel.

He **WAS** the only game in town and took it to the extreme. His workers were overworked and underpaid. They believed that because he was making so much money, he should "share the wealth."

And so it began . . .

I won't bother with a history lesson about the advent of workforce unionization. You can see the results for yourself.

Refocus. You must clearly understand that employee compensation is a *business* transaction. As the owner of that business you alone will determine this:

**How much money is going to GO in and STAY IN your pocket?**

Your employee or future employee has everything **BUT** that, at the forefront of their mind.

They don't care about you.

Sorry to say that, but it is true.

YOU are a necessary evil for them. *YOU* are their adversary. And frankly, that is good. There needs to be a very clearly drawn line in the sand that identifies who is boss and who is not.

So the idea is to keep as much profit as we can, what we pay, and how do we do it.

I am not going to tell you what to pay, as you should base that on your industry standards. And I've already told you that I will pay *more* for the right person.

Myself and John are highly paid consultants for good reason . . . We're good . . . REAL good. Sure, you could find many people cheaper, but not anywhere near the value we bring. Price and value are two different things.

You can find out about our business consulting programs at www.sendinthewolves.com.

This approach will be helpful in determining your pay scale. Don't give away the store, but don't miss the long-term benefit and intangibles the right person can bring to the table.

I also strongly recommend that you pay very generous, performance and results base bonuses.

Note I said "performance and results based."

Most employees at some point develop an entitlement rather than an ownership mentality, feeling that time served and company profits should correlate into more money for them, earned or not. You see this with unions and especially the teachers union.

I also recommend public recognition of a job well done. Everyone likes a good pat on the back every once in a while especially when it is in front of others. Good for the ego.

You may think that this is counter to what I said earlier about having a no nonsense work place but it isn't. To be profitable, you don't need to run a sweatshop or be a dictator.

What you do want is to run your business with a firm hand and clear guidelines.

Your employees work better when they are allowed to excel, be recognized, appreciated, and rewarded for it. You do this because they *earned* it.

The employee/owner relationship is adversarial enough without them hating your guts because you do not appreciate their *good* work. Sometimes a good pat on the back and an "atta-boy" will go a long way.

## CHAPTER 21 – JIM TONER

---

# Partnerships

*Partnership is the worst ship to sail.*

~Jims Father-In-Law

Aye matey, and so it is.

What is the phrase the kids use today? OMG!

Yeah, OMG. I could write some scary stuff in this chapter, but I'll try and keep it tame in an effort for all you out there with a partner from taking a bridge.

It's a funny thing how everyone seems to feel that they need partners when going into business for themselves. I guess it's a security issue; meaning an internal security.

That is not a knock on anyone as I was dumb enough to do it incorrectly not once, but twice!

I will put this as simply as I can:

192

**DON'T DO IT** *unless you know* **HOW.**

Seriously, don't do it. My big mistake in the failed partnerships I had is the same mistake that many entrepreneurs make. We tend to look at people and situations not as they truly are, but as we would like them to be.

In my case, I had always been a very trusting person. Take note of my use of the past tense "had."

In the past, I liked to believe what people told me. I liked to believe they would do nothing to harm me. And I liked to believe that they were as competent as they told me they were. All of the above and much more, came back to bite me on my two failed attempts.

I say "bite", but *eviscerate* may be more accurate.

I am not going to get into the gory details but I will tell you that it cost me hundreds of thousands of dollars as well as very close relationships because of these partnerships. It was only AFTER I discovered how partnerships should be structured that I met with success.

The truth about partnerships is that they rarely succeed, and I mean rarely.

I know, I know, YOU are one of those rarities.

(I hope you are, but I highly doubt it.)

With this in mind, if you are not already in a partnership, it is best to plan for the breakup before it happens. I will discuss later what to do if you are already in the trap . . . I mean, partnership.

---

## The Rules

Whenever we begin a new business venture, it's kind of like that new girlfriend or boyfriend. Everything is great and everything is going to stay great.

Right?

That is how we naturally tend to look at things; especially entrepreneurs who are naturally *over*-optimistic. And we hope that turns out to be the case.

But, in business as is in life, sometimes things go sideways.

What that means is *you know what* hits the fan. That is what you need to be ready for. Can you picture in your mind what's happening?

Yeah.

It's messy and all over everyone. Where do you think that phrase came from? So we start with *clear* expectations and rules that will be spelled out in what is known as an Operating Agreement.

If there were a Ten Commandments of business, and I am sure that somewhere there probably is, one of the ten would have to be.

## THOU SHALL NOT EVER, EVER, ENGAGE IN ANY TYPE OF PARTNERSHIP WITHOUT AN OPERATING AGREEMENT

The results of ignoring this commandment can and most likely will be ugly.

Trust me, I know.

An Operating Agreement basically contains the rules of the company. It spells out who is responsible for what, who gets what and what happens when we fall out of love and or someone screws up real bad and we want to dissolve the company and/or partnership.

You already know that I don't like using attorneys. But, as much as I hate using them, I recommend that for this, you use one.

You and your partner can sit down in advance and lay out some ground rules and have your attorney can help with the rest. On a side note, always do as much work as possible yourself instead of letting an attorney start from scratch.

I am warning you.

Begging you.

*Threatening* you

**DO NOT** go into any business partnership without this agreement. When the time comes that it is clear things are not working and you need to get out.

You need to get out . . . and fast.

Be sure that you have any dissolution clause be made **VERY** clear, as this will help buffer the animosity and negativity that will occur. Get out as professionally and cleanly as possible.

Don't get into a battle.

**When it's over: IT IS OVER!**

Do whatever you have to do to get out in one piece. Are you wondering why I started with the end? Don't worry, you can thank me later.

---

### Things to Consider

Now that I have probably convinced you that your partnership is going to end in disaster, let's talk about how to prevent that from happening. As I said, the Operating Agreement defines the rules of the company.

We talked about getting out. Let's talk about getting in. Here are a few things to consider before you finalize your partnership with anyone:

1. Who owns what? If you are smart, you will fight and fight very hard for majority ownership of your new company. This also applies in any type of joint venture or merger. You should always want to maintain the upper hand in the ownership department. I would start at demanding 75% ownership. Yes, demand it. Scream for it. Fight for it. It *IS* that important. Never, and I mean *never*, do the standard 50/50. Take 51% if you have to, but never below that.

2. What are they, the potential partners, bringing to the table? Money, talent, connections? Far too many people go into business with friends, fami-

ly members, and/or acquaintances without taking a hard look at what they have that is going to put more money in your pocket. If you were going to start a new NFL team, would you go out and grab the first bunch of guys who said they wanted to play or, would you go out and scout some already proven players and pick from the best? Right? So why be any different with your biz? By the way, in a partnership, making money comes first so I would advise that any relationship you wish to keep intact does not become part of your biz. Money's one thing, friends and family are another.

3. Are the skill and or talents they bring different from yours? This is very important. You do not need a clone of yourself; you need someone who complements what you have or brings something you do not have.

4. Can they take the heat? The reality of business is that it is tough. No way around it. So can this person or persons take it when this occurs? How will they react? Do they have any past history that you can give you a look into how they may perform under fire, i.e. "stress"? You may have heard the phrase that had its origins in military circles, "I wouldn't want to be caught in a foxhole with you." This means, in the heat of the

battle, back against the wall, would you want that person in your foxhole? Could you trust them to fight and have your back?

5. How "IN" are they? Dedication is always bandied about when talking about success. It is however, very true. In this ultra-competitive world, you better damn well be **VERY** dedicated and laser focused.

Early on I had a partner who brought a lot to the table He was also a lifelong friend. He was a moneymaker, aggressive, and smart. He also had a passion to become a pilot. Eventually, that passion won out and forced us to remove him from the company resulting in lawsuits and lost friendships. There is no halfway in.

---

**The Big Five**

So, you have your five things to consider before a partnership, now, here are the five items that MUST be included in your operating agreement.

1. Salaries / Distributions. This is just what you think it is. How much are we getting paid, when, and how is it being done.

2. Buy in. Otherwise known as CAPITAL CONTRIBUTION. Hey, you've got to pay to play baby. No

free rides. Each member must make a Capital Contribution to get into the company.

3. <u>Decision making.</u> This is a biggie. Obviously, many decisions will be made on a daily basis and most people always think that their answer is the best. You need to have this in writing. Who is calling the shots? If decisions are being made by committee, which I hate, what is the process?

4. <u>Death or disability of a partner</u>. In the event one or more of the partners bite the dust, you need to have a plan in place to be able to keep moving forward should you choose to do so.

5. <u>Dissolution.</u> This is the end game and it must be planned before played.

---

**Ready for a Shootout?**

In the event that you choose not to listen to me and decide to do a 50/50, *AT LEAST* be smart enough to include the following in your operating agreement.

Believe me when I tell you that when you need to get out or rid of someone, it needs to happen and happen fast. So what we are going to do is include an exit strategy known as a Mexican Shootout. Sounds cool doesn't it?

Here is how it works:

- When things go sideways, or you fall out of love with each other, or you realize your partner is a lazy cash-sucking slob and you both want to get as far away from each other as possible, this baby will kick in.

- Each partner will write a figure on a piece of paper, (privately) and place it in a sealed envelope. *This figure is what you would be willing to pay for the ENTIRE Company*, and you or they must have access to the amount you have chosen as your figure.

- The envelopes are brought to a neutral attorney where they will be opened.

- Whoever has bid the highest amount is now the owner of the Company, and must pay the loser for their shares based on figure indicated in the losers sealed bid.

You need to be very careful and closely consider your figure before you put it on paper. This clause is not for the squeamish but it does bring things to a very quick and final end. On the flip side, you may end up with something you don't want.

So let's say you choose this route and the "winner" does not have the buyout funds. It would be a good idea to set a timeline in your agreement for how long of a grace period will be given. If the "winner" is still not able to come up with the cash in the allotted timeline, the other partner will have the option to buy at his offered amount.

Just as is the case with a real shootout, the end is quick. However, the partner without access to funding resources could be at a disadvantage.

## Mediation

Here is another potential solution to resolving your partnership conflict, although I personally find it to only be effective if the people involved are *truly* interested in resolving things.

Basically, you and the partner(s) will sit with a neutral party, which is usually an attorney, and the attorney will hear both sides of the argument and attempt to mediate. I have been involved in this type of situation twice with the results being 50/50.

## Worst Case Scenario

I am well aware that many things in life are far worse than a bad business deal, but being in a partnership, with no agreement, and needing to get out or get rid of someone, ranks pretty high up there. The financial and mental toll it can and will take is pretty big.

So what can you do if you are in the situation with a partner and no agreement? This is a tough one simply because there are no painless answers.

Here are a few options:

1. If you *really* want to keep the business going but *really* need to get rid of your partner(s), you can offer to buy them out. Not pretty as they will probably want far more than you can or are willing to pay.

2. Or, they can buy you out. Again, not painless as it will force you to start over and perhaps lose hard earned reputation and/or customers.

3. You can stick it out, swallow your pride, and try and keep it together. I don't really recommend this method. When you know you have cancer, you need to cut it out.

4. You can file a lawsuit. I have done this, again I don't recommend it. I am not saying you can't or won't win. What I am saying is that the real winner will be the attorneys. Most people vastly underestimate the time and money involved in a lawsuit. You will pay a high price with both.

5. You can just walk. Just say forget it, it's not worth my time, health, sanity, etc. Leave. Go. Split. Ske-

daddle. . . GTFO . . . however you want to put it, just get out. In many, many cases, this is the best way to go. Money is very replaceable while time and your sanity is not.

---

## Your Best Solution

As NIKE says, "Just do it."

Jimmy says, "Just DON'T do it."

In today's day and age having a partner that brings BIG game to the table can be huge, but in most cases, you can go it alone. You can have advisors or key people, but partners can be avoided

Whether you know it or not, everything you need to run a successful business is already at your fingertips. You can outsource just about everything you need and have employees, if necessary, for the rest.

Of all of the most successful people I know, very few of them have a partner and many that did learned the hard way.

I just told you what to do.

The question is . . .

Will you listen to me?

# Time, Time, Tickin', Tickin' Away...

Aah yes . . . Time Management.

Actually, it should be called Time **MIS**-management.

Time doesn't need to be managed.

You do.

So, where to begin? I know. How about a simple quiz?

Are you ready? This question is worth 100 points . . .

How many hours are in a day?

"Well duh, Jim. Obviously 24."
Hmmm, OK, very good.

So it seems that the problem here is not that you do not know how many hours you have available in a day. The problem is that you have no idea what to do with them, right?

Oh, I know you *think* you know what to do, but you probably don't. And if by some chance you do, why are you not doing it?

Here's why.

You're surfing the web, talking to friends, thinking about yesterday, thinking about tomorrow, answering your phone, texting, listening to the radio, watching TV, driving around, picking your nose, kicking a can down the street . . . blah, blah, blah.

Yes, I am going to be a bit harsher in this chapter. I can't stand to hear someone say they have "no time" or, "There just aren't enough hours in a day," or, "I just don't know where all the time goes."

As Frank Sinatra used to say, "Don't make me slug you, punk."

We *ALL* have the same amount of time. 24 hours a day.

That's it.

You know that, you passed your quiz. But that's not the issue. The issue is how you *spend* your time, so let me try and walk you through this process of "time management."

We have all heard the expression, "Time is Money," right? Well, it is. So your first step is to determine, how much you are worth.

I mean really, what *IS* your time worth?

- Eight dollars an hour?
- Twenty dollars an hour?
- One hundred dollars an hour?
- One thousand dollars an hour?

I can't tell you what *your* hourly rate should be but I can tell you that any of the above mentioned, time-wasting activities will probably not put you very high on any pay scale.

Actually, for business purposes, *any* activity that is not directly leading you in some manner to profit is completely worthless. And when you honestly think about how much of your time you really spend on these worthless activities, I would hope it would hurt just a bit.

If you want to be in the $1,000.00 an hour range, you need to be doing activities that make you worthy of that type of dough. Rest assured that anyone making high six or seven figures is **NOT** spending their days on time/money sucking activities.

"But Jim, it's so hard. You kind of just get sucked into it." Yeah, I know.

You want to find out what burned down, who died, and what Kim Kardashian did last night.

Hey, if that's your thing, have at it. Just don't expect the big dollar signs to come your way.

*(Speaking of Kim Kardashian, say what you want about her, but you better believe that she spends every waking moment figuring out how to make more cash. She is not spending her days surfing the web wasting time. She is working very hard to get all the cash she can from the legion of drones following her every move. If you want something valuable from watching her, watch how she markets herself.)*

So the trick here is not to get sucked into the time vacuum in the first place. And here is how we do it.

The late, great Jim Rohn had a *very* powerful quote regarding time management. He said, "Don't start your day before you finish it."

Did you get that? Think about it now . . .

What he is saying is don't start your day until you pre-plan what the day is going to look like. You need to do this the night or day or week before and *not* when you wake up on said day.

So whatever method of activity tracking you prefer or use, whether it be a Day-Timer, computer, whatever, you must plan your days and weeks in advance. Doing this allows you to know exactly what you should be doing and when. If followed correctly, meaning in a disciplined manner, it will also help prevent any of the so-called interruptions that leave you saying, "There aren't enough hours in the day."

What I do is prioritize things in order of importance. No rocket science there. Lots of gurus have bandied this about. What you need to do is the same. What are the *most* important items that need to be accomplished that day? Please be clear on the word *most* important.

## *Tip: Add Deadlines!*

Surfing the web to check the latest dirt is not going to generate profit for you. But, how about upon awakening, spending thirty minutes reading a book on sales, marketing, or better yet, *this* book?

I've talked to tons of people who wonder how some people get so much done while others get nothing done.

Again, not rocket science.

## *They are the masters of their time.*

It seems like such a simple idea, doesn't it, planning your day in advance. Prioritizing activities in order of importance, putting deadlines on tasks, etc.

Sounds good.

Sounds easy too, but as Mike Tyson once said, "Everybody has plan until they get punched in the face." Well said, Champ.

If that is the case, and it is, what is "punching us in the face" and how do we stop it?

Let's evaluate Jim' top eight reasons people are *not* the masters of their time:

---

### Reason #1. The Phone/Cellphone

I swear I remember a time when there was no such thing as a cell phone, and I'm pretty sure I made money back then.

Now? Good God, forget your phone and the world ends. You are, after all, a very important person and you must be able to be reached at all times. Aah no. You're not *that* important. At least not so important that you need to be accessible every second of the day.

The scary thing about the phone is that it has brainwashed us into thinking everything that is happening is urgent in nature and we must be readily available. When was the last time you tried to go twenty-four hours without touching your phone for anything other than *scheduled* calls? How often during the day do you find yourself in the middle of an activity and you stop because your phone rings?

Even worse, how often are you meeting with someone and *their* phone rings and they stop to answer? Here is a tip for you and perhaps a warning. I will not conduct business with someone who does that. If we have a meeting set, and my time is very expensive and very scarce and someone stops to pick up a phone?

We are done. Why?

Because just like someone being consistently late, that is a sign that they do not respect your time.

Hey, if you don't respect my time . . . bye-bye.

As I alluded to, the only phone calls you should be taking, if you are interested in maximum productivity, are "scheduled" calls.

If you have a secretary and or receptionist, that is a good start. Not only can they make sure that calls are scheduled, but they can be the all-important *gatekeeper* who shields you from unwanted and unneeded interruptions.

Your *gatekeeper* can be given a list of calls that will be accepted should they come in. Remember, you're not **that** important, so be careful not to decide to take every call.

## PRIORITIZE to MONETIZE!

Believe it or not, I just thought of that phrase.

Not bad, and also very true.

All other calls coming in **not** on the *hot* list can be dismissed, redirected, or scheduled for the future.

All this stuff is easy if you would just implement it.

Unless you are in phone sales, I see no reason for anyone to be held hostage by the phone, whether willingly or unwillingly.

Here is a valuable tip for you.

The reason most people are addicted to the phone is they feel they will "miss" something or "lose" a deal or business.

The reality is this. Your clients and the public can easily be conditioned to follow the rules that *you* set forth. Believe it or not, you can actually tell people when you accept calls and when you will return calls. You can also tell them what "type" of calls will or will not be accepted. You can also tell them that you *never* accept incoming calls unless pre-scheduled.

Guess what?

For the most part, they will listen.

*Stop* worrying about missing something or upsetting someone. Train people to adapt to the way you want to do business. It really is that simple.

---

## Reason #2: The Internet

Wow, that thing is a mousetrap if there ever was one. Crack cocaine has got nothing on the internet.

Frankly, I am still in a bit of turmoil over the internet.

On one hand, it is an awesome source of instant information. When you think about the time that can be saved and the resources you have at your disposal it is pretty impressive.

Now on the *other* hand, it can be and frequently is the biggest time suck ever created. I don't know the exact stats, but I know that a frighteningly large amount of time is spent by average workers spend surfing the web, *on their boss's dime!*

To me, that is no different than theft.

And if you're the boss and you are spending your time on the web, you're stealing from yourself.

I am of the opinion that there is a mass brainwashing of the population taking place.

I am not alone in this opinion.

This brainwashing, being conducted by government, media, and the web, more specifically Google, is designed to drive your thoughts and action to the avenues of their bidding.

From a cultural standpoint, I find it to be horrifying.
From a business standpoint, I find it to be potentially fatal.

Google's slogan of "Don't do evil" is way beyond laughable. They are one of the dirtiest, sneakiest players in the game and they want *your* money. They know that when they get your attention, they can get your money.

Every minute you spend online that doesn't directly correspond with your business is money out of your pocket. If you gave an honest assessment of how much time you waste each day online and on the phone, I think you might be stunned.

I hope so at least.

If you are in an online business, which many people are, go ahead have at it.

If you are not, you need to keep yourself in check.

I promise you, if something *big* happens, you will find out.

You don't need to have your face buried online all day.

---

## Reason #3: Unscheduled Interruptions

The term is *Time Vampires*.

I'm sure you've heard that before but if not, I am sure you get it. This is more frequent within an office setting, especially if you are the boss.

Everyone wants you for five minutes, "Really, Boss, just five minutes." The problem is everyone's five minutes add up fast. I'm amused by the "open door policy" being implemented by so many organizations.

Open doors mean open season in my book.

Open season on *your* time.

I strongly recommend that you have a very clear policy with your employees regarding their access to you and your time. This is easier with smaller companies but also easily accomplished with larger companies as well.

I am a big fan of the "closed door" policy.

When your door is closed, you can focus on what is really important, which is marketing your business. And this is where the majority of your time *should* be spent.

If, however, you are of the "open door" philosophy at least control the situation. If you are going to allow someone to walk into your office, unscheduled, asking for "just five minutes," here is what I suggest.

First, ask the level of importance of the issue. Let them know that your day is packed and you can only deal with issues that are a 9 or 10 on a scale of 1 to 10. Ask them directly, "Is this a 9 or 10?"
Put it back on them.

Make them think twice before taking your time. Any issues that are not on that level can be put off until later.
Next, ask if this issue can be dealt with by anyone other than you.

If there *is* only you, be sure the issue is a 9 or 10. I also want them to bring not only the issue, but a potential solution. You want your employees to be able to think for themselves and not have to bug you with things they should be able to handle on their own. You need them to understand that they have permission to deal with certain issues.

So, don't bring a problem without a solution.

Lastly, if they "must" have five minutes, then they have *just* five minutes. That's it, five minutes.

People use five minutes as more of an expression than an actual timeline. Unless otherwise directed, five minutes is rarely five minutes. So if someone needs the five minutes, we set the clock. "This sounds so mean, Jim." No, it sounds smart.

Get to the crux of the issue, without any filler, and move on. It is as simple as that.

This also applies to your employees. "Water cooler" talk should be renamed, "Bleed my bank account talk." When employees are "shooting the breeze" they are not doing what they are being paid to do. (Please refer back to the employee chapter and re-read the Measure and Manage part.)

Any managers, middle managers, administrative assistants or anyone in a position where people will want to talk with them, need to implement the above strategy. I am not discounting any issues that are below a 9 or 10, I am just saying that those can be delegated or pushed back. Many times those issues are, and should be, dealt with by the managers or middle managers.

---

## Reason #4: Meetings

There is a reason for the phrase, "Death by Meeting."

This is very similar to Reason #3 above and the solution is very similar too. I hate meetings and I make it very clear to anyone who wants a meeting with me that I hate meetings.

I also make it clear that there will be a very clear agenda and timeline and neither of these will be altered.

I understand that there is certainly a time and place for meetings. I understand the importance of meetings. I also clearly understand the misuse of meetings.

Our society has become so dependent on hand-holding that you need to have a meeting about going to the bathroom.

So, if and when you are going to have a meeting, here are the guidelines:

- Set a clear start and finish time and do not waver from it.

- Make sure everyone involved is aware of this.

- Next be sure to have clear agenda that you are ready to tackle immediately upon the start of the meeting.

- Keep a clock in a prominent place and make sure everyone is well aware of the time remaining.

- Food and or drinks are a bad idea unless this is a multi-hour or day-long planning session.

There you have it. Seems simple because it is.

That being said, I would like to recommend a great book on meetings called *Mastering the Rockefeller Habits* by Verne Harnish. This book gives you all the info you will ever need to know about meetings.

## Reason #5: Lack of Urgency

This may seem out of place in a Time Management section but it is actually right at home.

One of the biggest time sucks you have is your own lack of urgency.

I am not sure when or how it happened, but these days it seems that many people are just leisurely cruising through life with the, "I'll get to it when I get to it attitude." Sorry to pop your bubble, but you'll sing that tune all the way to the poor house. There is an expression that says, "Fortune favors the Bold."

Yes, it does. It also favors the speedy.

A gazelle on the Serengeti in Africa cannot afford to be slow and lazy. A gazelle is prey for the lions. You, my friend, will be the gazelle in business with an attitude that is anything less than urgent. You will, like a careless gazelle, be slaughtered.

The "truth" is that none of us know when our hourglass will run out. The "problem" is that many people think it never will. Oh, but it will. As I write this chapter, my mother-in-law, whom I love, is battling Alzheimer's. I cannot begin to tell you what a wicked disease it is and would not wish it on my worst enemy.

The torment she and my father-in-law are going through is heartbreaking. They both know that it's over. They also know that they unfortunately wasted much of the time that they did have. It's too late now.

Don't go to that place. You won't like it.

Don't fool yourself into thinking you have tomorrow.

Maybe you do, maybe you don't.

What you have is today, that's it.

You need to develop a "grab life by the throat attitude" and operate as if there really is no tomorrow, because there may not be. I promise you that life will give you what you want, but there is a price. The price, however, for getting what you truly want is the best deal in town.

The price for sloth, you cannot afford.

Operate with urgency.

---

## Reason #6: Email (See Phone and Internet)

Yes, another ball and chain keeping you from your pot of gold. Hopefully, you remember when we did not have email. Remember that?

I would be willing to bet that you functioned quite well. This is nothing more than another method of someone wanting to take you to his or her product or service. On the personal side, it is not much different than someone walking into your office for that "Just five minutes" deal.

Email has its place.

But, just like most drugs it is, more often than not, abused. You **do not** need to check your email every five minutes. As I said earlier, no offense, you are not that important and anything of *real* importance you will find out about sooner or later.

Back off.

I actually know a few *very* rich and *very* successful individuals who refuse to use email.

They understand that their fortunes were made before the advent of email and while it may be a convenience, it is not a necessity to operating your business. As in the case with cell phones, as a society, we have become conditioned to keeping the umbilical cord plugged in.

Yes, *conditioned*!

222

Keep the email-checking to once or twice a day, not 100 times a day. I promise, you will survive. If you're concerned that customers will be upset, simply inform them that you only check your emails once a day.

## TRAIN YOUR CUSTOMERS AND DISCIPLINE YOURSELF

And as far as you being the one blasting people with email?

## NEWS FLASH!

Most emails are deleted without being read. If you really want someone's attention, nothing beats a great direct mail piece. Remember that, direct mail? Yeah, it's the next big thing that never left.

---

**Reason #7: All Social Media**

More and more I am beginning to feel like I am in the land of the walking dead. Social Media has got to be the biggest waste of time ever to see the light of day. Even Rubik's Cube makes you think. Not social media. If anything, it dumbs you down *fast.* I am not going to waste any time going off on a personal rant against this trash but if I did, it would be a good one. For sure I would offend lots of Face Bookers and Tweeters. I will save that fun for another day.

From a productivity standpoint, sorry, I just don't see it.

I very strongly believe that the value placed on social media as a business vehicle, is *grossly* overvalued. As with some of the other things mentioned, I am not saying that there is no place for it, but I am saying the actual level of value it brings to you personally and on the business front does not match the hype. From a productivity standpoint . . . **ZERO.** I'm sure that there are many who would disagree with me on this, probably the same people telling us what they had to eat last night or what they did five minutes ago, but . . .

When discussing employees, I frequently used the terms, Measure and Manage. It is no different here.

If you can measure something, you can determine the probable outcomes. I have worked with many business owners who have bought into the social media business and services marketing B.S. and gave it a real shot. I mean they really worked diligently, with a good plan and budget. Nothing half-assed. They also closely monitored the progress. To a person, their determination was that social media was a complete waste of time and money as a sole or main advertising vehicle. Every so-called marketing wiz out there wants to sell you on the power of social media for your biz.

I'll tell you what. Have them pay for it and see how enthused they are.

---

**Reason #8: Television**

Let's say you go out and buy yourself a nice big ole' top of the line 900" plasma television that is bound to impress not only the entire neighborhood but even the good Lord himself. As this is now your pride and joy, you can't wait to have folks over to show them this Eighth Wonder of the World. After all the oohs and aahs, someone says, "Wow, how much did that cost?" You proudly say, "I paid $4,300.00 for that baby."

(I'm making these numbers up gang, work with me.)

So, here is the real question.

Is that *really* how much it cost? Yes, that may be how much you paid, but is that what it cost?

Are you following me?
Sure, you paid $4,300.00, which was the *price*. The cost, however, is *far* more.

Why?

Well my guess is that unfortunately you may be spending far too much time in front of your new pride and joy. This is time that you will never get back and time that could have and *should* have been spent on more productive activities.

When you add up the time *lost* watching television and equate that into dollars, you will see that you may have overpaid just a bit.

Hey, I am not saying that you should never watch TV. I enjoy watching the ball games just like everyone else.

What I am saying is that most people spend an average of three hours a day watching television. That is twenty-one hours a week. It is a whopping 1,092 hours a year. If you valued your time at only $20.00 an hour, that is $21,840.00 a year out of your pocket. You may scoff and say. "Well, that's not a lot of money."

Really?

I have a feeling if I walked up to you with a check for twenty grand in my hand you would not be scoffing.

Listen, just be smart. Don't get sucked into the mass brainwashing. If you want to spend a few hours a week in front of the set, fine, have at it. Just remember though, it comes with a price, and that price is *not* what you paid for the thing.

I suppose that I could continue to list any number of activities that are time-wasters, but those are the main ones. I'm sure by now you've gotten the point. When you have clearly defined objectives that need to be accomplished, you simply eliminate anything that does not add to getting said tasks done.

I know that sounds very simple.

Why?

Because it IS!

Here, let's make it even easier by quoting Nike, "JUST DO IT."

---

## Where and When to Work

When you are talking about maximum productivity, it is super important to operate in conditions that are favorable to you. The two main conditions I am talking about are:

- *Time*
- *Surroundings*

Let's start with time.

227

As I am sure you can see, there are a number of recurring themes in this book. One of them is how people have been conditioned to fit someone else's agenda.

From a *time* standpoint, we have been conditioned to wake at certain times, work during certain times, eat during certain times, and so on.

This is a mistake.

Time can be very flexible in many cases. Most entrepreneurs and business owners have certain "peak" times of the day when they are most effective. Before I discovered this I used to think that there was something wrong with me.

I would be *very* productive early in the morning and mid-morning. And then between, one and three in the afternoon I would just be useless and not very motivated. Right after three in the afternoon, I'm back on it. It has been very useful to me to understand that you need not conform to so-called, "traditional work hours."

---

## Determine Your Peak Working Times

*Where* you are putting in your time is a very important component to time management. It may not seem to be on the surface, but if you look closer, you will find that most people do not operate to their full potential when the environment is less than stellar. In other words . . . it sucks.

When at all possible, put yourself in a position to do your work in an environment that inspires you. For instance, as I write this chapter I am sitting on the back patio of my Scottsdale, Arizona home. I live in the desert, which is beautiful enough, but I have a million dollar view of the mountains too. Other times I will go to Janeys Coffee in Cave Creek and write. Cool place with a great vibe and great music.

Again, *very* easy to be productive in a good environment.

Should you be in a position to work wherever you want, I strongly recommend you find a place where you can not only be less stressed, but more productive.

If you happen to be landlocked and cannot really work remotely, be sure to make the space you have a creative, inspiring environment.

In my old home in Pittsburgh, I had my office set up in such a manner that you could not help but be inspired, i.e. more productive.

My bookshelves had hundreds of books. (I read them all by the way.) Pictures of Carnegie, Lincoln, and Henry Ford covered my walls. I had awards I had won and testimonial letters from clients. I actually felt smarter just walking into the room.

The point is that no matter where you are you can create a space that will help you be more inspired. And yes, that has a lot to do with time management.

## Some Additional Thoughts

- Be very careful of associations. I will cover this later but just beware of the potential productivity suck this can be. People, employees, etc.

- When you can, work from home. The commute time is a bit more favorable.

- Say NO more often. Many people are people pleasers and being such feel bad about telling someone no. Again, this is *YOUR* time being stripped away to fill someone else's agenda.

- Work non-stop when the time is right. As I said earlier, there will be times when you find yourself at peak activity. Sometimes however, you will find yourself in what is well known as "the ZONE" This is when you are "out of your mind" unstoppable. When you are in that space . . . keep going. When I am writing for example, sometimes I can only get out five or so pages before I am trailing off. Other times however, I can knock out fifty pages without batting an eye. When you're on a roll, keep rolling.

- Stop making excuses. Another one that may seem odd for time management but if you think about, how many people do you know, and maybe know *very* well, who spend hours complaining about anything and everything. Listen, life is not fair and there are no guarantees. Get over it. Create the world you want. Stop wasting time complaining about things you cannot control.

- Set deadlines. Deadlines are a wonderful creation, unless of course you are going to miss yours. Put yourself under the gun and set a deadline. When I set out to write this book I didn't say that I needed to write 300 pages in one day. What I did was say to myself that giving myself three months from start to finish. I then broke that down to daily and weekly tasks that needed to be completed. It is also helpful to put yourself on the hook with others as far as completion timelines.

- Delegate. As entrepreneurs we always feel we need to "do it all." Well, you don't and you shouldn't. The reality is that you will probably screw up most of it anyway. The Mastermind Principal from *Think and Grow Rich* by Napoleon Hill is probably the greatest success concept ever created.

Other people's time, talent and money. Focus only on what you are the very best at and delegate the rest.

# Uh-Oh...

As the old saying goes, sometimes "shit happens."
We don't want it to, but it does, in every business and to everyone.  The reality in life and in business is that sometimes, things just don't work out.

What do you do when your business venture is not working out?

Unfortunately, the odds are stacked against many of you, especially if you are trying to feel your way through things, which, by the way, makes this book worth a million dollars to you if you're smart.

Let me break this down in order of procedure on what to do if you are in the danger zone so you're not flopping around like a fish out of water.

The first thing you need to do is to *accurately* assess the degree of the issue.  Is it just day-to-day, pain-in-the-butt business issues or is it the stake through the heart?

## Chicken Little

It is easy to panic and overreact when everything is on your head. You start to think that the world is coming to an end and you are going down with it. It's very easy to get caught up in that. That, however, is not going to be very productive. You won't think clearly and you may make rash decisions that make things worse.

Listen, the truth is that it's only money we are talking about here.

Money is VERY replaceable. Don't get overly rattled about minor issues.

So Number One is to assess.

If the issue is not a deathblow, take a step back and rationally look at what the issue is and what needs to be done to get rid of it. I'm assuming, of course, you really want to continue in business. I understand that this may be easier said than done when you're trying to meet payroll but it needs to be done nonetheless.

Look at the issue for what it *really* is and not the horror story you are probably creating in your head.

## What IS the Problem?

If it is a cash flow issue, which is the case with many small business owners, determine exactly how deep that hole is. Remember, it is critical that you have "accurate thinking" on this. Actually, accurate thinking is one of the key principals in Napoleon Hill's *Think and Grow Rich*.

As the saying goes, "It is what it is."

Gather your key financial person and crunch numbers. If you are the sole financial guy, grab your accountant and some booze . . . just kidding about the booze. It is also very helpful to bring someone in who is not as emotionally involved as you, especially when it comes to money.

Dig deep and find out IF you can get out of the crisis and if so, how do you do it . . . step by step.

You would be amazed what a good plan can do as opposed to flying by the seat of your pants.

Yes, I'm talking to you.

Put together a plan. Can you negotiate any debts, get more sales, collect past due receivables, etc.? You really need to throw everything you've got against the wall and see what sticks. Depending on your type of business, sometimes you are only a few sales away from getting back on your feet. So don't panic, yet, and look at the real hard numbers.

---

## Find the REAL Issue

Remember this saying, "Math doesn't lie, people do." The numbers will either work or they won't.

What if it is not a cash flow problem? Frankly, if it is not a cash flow problem, you really don't have what I consider a *major* problem, unless you are involved in criminal activity or a regulatory agency is breathing down your neck.

Death of your cash flow is really the only thing that can permanently kill your biz.

Maybe it's an employee issue? I hope I made my point on that subject but in case I didn't, go back and re-read.

If you got a bad one . . . GET RID OF IT.

Yes, I said IT.

I have zero respect for deliberately bad employees who take advantage of the good will and finances of business owners.

Regulatory issues? Guess what?

Big Brother *IS* watching and watching *VERY* closely.

This could be an issue. If you think that Government agencies and regulatory bodies are the good guys out to protect the unsuspecting public from the big bad wolf, no pun intended, you're wrong. Very wrong.

They, my friends, are some of if not *THE* dirtiest players in the game. And when you are dealing with bad guys the rulebook goes out the window, at least for them.

Just to give you an idea on how deep this goes, I have personally had a regulatory agency tell me that a *LEGAL AND BINDING CONTRACT*, written by attorneys, and signed of free will by an individual...

*DOES NOT MATTER.*

As I said: if they want you, they make the rules.

Some of this will be repeated in the "bonus" legal chapter but it surely does bear repeating. If you are in a situation where your business is up against the government and or a regulatory body, you *MUST* get very, very good representation. As much as I do not like to use attorneys, sometimes it is a must, and this is one of those times.

If this is a BBB (Better Business Bureau) issue or something of that nature, you can deal with it on your own. Anything else, bring in the big dogs. Whoever you bring in **MUST** be well versed in these issues. You need to remember the beast you are dealing with. They have no rules. Think I am kidding?

I have a very good friend by the name of Bill Bartmann who, at one point, was worth 1.1 **BILLION** dollars and was the twenty-fifth wealthiest person in the United States. The government, led by Attorney General John Ashcroft, came after him on trumped up charges of insider trading. He was facing over 200 years in prison!! He fought and he won, but they sent him into bankruptcy.

Over 3,000 people lost their jobs and he lost everything he had. The government sent him a letter of apology when they discovered his innocence.

Yeah, it's that serious.

On the flip side, Bill, who is one of the greatest entrepreneurial stories in history, had a comeback. Once again he is a multi-millionaire AND he and his company have been nominated for the Nobel Peace Prize in 2014.

Not too bad. Yes, there can be a comeback.

So, back to what to do if Big Brother is after you . . . get great counsel, and keep your mouth **SHUT**. It is **VERY** tempting to mouth off when you know you have done nothing wrong and are being attacked, but you need to keep a lid on it. Let you counsel deal with it, keep your head down and try to survive.

If, on the other hand, what you did was intentionally criminal in nature. You're on your own and I hope they get you. As a matter of fact, throw this book out; you're not anyone I want to be around.

---

## Time to Sell

One more thing to consider if you are in deep water is selling your business.

You would be surprised how many people are out there that may be willing to buy potentially viable businesses. You may have some unseen assets that may be very valuable to someone else. A good customer list for example.

The point is you need to explore all options when in a hole.

So what if the biz cannot be saved? What if you have determined that there is no way out of the jam you're in? Well my friend, you will not be the first and surely will not be the last to bite the dust. I could fill two pages of legendary figures who have filed bankruptcy; some of whom have filed multiple times.

It ain't pretty, and it ain't painless, but it also ain't fatal or permanent.

Trust me, I know. I shared my story earlier, If you need to file bankruptcy, get it done and get back on the horse.

As I said, it's only money, paper with dead presidents on it.

That's it.

There is lots of money out there just waiting for you to go and pick it up. This is not a *real* problem. Real problems are kids with cancer, or people starving, or any number of REAL problems.

Money is not one of them as long as you realize how easily replaceable it is.

So if you need to go down with the ship, go down. But as with any good captain, make sure you save as many people as you can before you go down. If you're going through a bankruptcy, some people are going to be hurt, just try your best to limit that number especially the "little" people. It's bad enough that you're in it, so keep the collateral damage to those who can least afford it to a minimum.

---

## Bankruptcy is NOT Failure

On a personal note, I want you to understand that a financial wipeout does *NOT* define who you are as a person.

We all tend to feel like failures and losers when this kind of thing happens but that is not the case. Yes, the business venture failed. Maybe your decision-making along the way helped speed this up. That doesn't mean you are a failure as a person. It's only money and its only business.

Like I said, better people than you have gone down in flames. Own it, but don't take it personally.

So now what? You're on your back looking up at the curb

.

Congratulations! Nowhere to go but up now.

Assuming of course that is your intention?

It is right?

**IF** you learned from your mistakes you are at a very big advantage to start again . . . with a clean slate for that matter.

Also during this time, it is critical that you feed your head with quality personal development material. You will be going through some dark days so you need to have information that will help you view things from a more positive prospective.

As they say, "This too shall pass."

. . . What are you waiting for?

# People Are Talking About You...

Oh yes they are! The million-dollar question is, "What are they saying?" When you break down a business to its simplest form, it's about attracting, capturing, and retaining customers. Obviously you need a good product or service to do this, but there is one component that I will say right now, will make or break you.

And here it is . . . *CUSTOMER SERVICE*!

You see, the reality is that if you do not have happy customers, you will have no business. With our current economy, keep this in the forefront of your mind.

Years ago, before the birth of the Internet, although you shouldn't have, you could have operated a business without too much concern about a few unhappy customers.

Business owners would get paid, the customer would be unhappy and the business owner would just say, "Next."

Unless you were very ethical, there was no major concern about a backlash that could put you out of business.

Sooooo . . . here we are today . . . the Internet age . . . there are no secrets.

Following the above scenario today, that unhappy customer gets online and lets the world know what a horrible business owner you are and that your product or service sucks.

Too many of these and you are out of business.

I have seen it happen over and over.

Bad news spreads like wildfire on the Internet and if you take advantage of a customer, look out. We will be covering in a later chapter the damage the Internet can cause, but for now, let's talk about how to prevent that from happening.

Let's talk about something that can make you and your business **VERY** successful.

Let's talk about the secret weapon for any business . . .

*RAVING FANS.*

Yes, raving fans!

Customers who are so blown away by your product and service that they want to tell everyone and their brother.

This *can* be done.

As a matter of fact, your business survival depends on it. Your competition is too tough to have it any other way.

Unfortunately, *many* business owners put this on the back burner. They take the money and say, "Next." That may work temporarily, but eventually, it will be your downfall. You **MUST** put customer service at the forefront of your business. And not just because it's the *right* thing to do, but because it's the *smart* thing to do.

You should not be selling a product or service that you are not totally proud of and you should never have the attitude that you do not care about the complete satisfaction of the customer. And I mean **NEVER**.

Some of you may already have this down. This may be second nature to you. However, my experience is that most business owners get a failing grade when it comes to customer service.

You are in business, I am assuming, to make money. You need to manage this as math. Happy customers come back, and tell lots of people. Unhappy customers don't come back . . . and tell lots of people.

You do the math.

How do we create this "Raving Fan"? When I look at my experiences with customer service, I think of Zappos, or Amazon both of which are widely known for their customer service. They are both the mega companies they are in large part **BECAUSE** of their customer service.

"But I'm not Zappos," you say. "I can't provide that level of service." Well, you're wrong. Remember the saying, "Little hinges swing big doors"?

You do not need to be a mega company to provide a **WOW** experience.

Beverly International is a bodybuilding supplement company based out of Cold Spring, Kentucky. They produce and sell bodybuilding supplements. I will go on record as saying that I believe they have the very best products in the world. I am, and have been, a long-time customer.

The key phrase there is, "long-time customer".

The question is why?

As great as their products are, that is only one part of the equation for their business success.

Remember, you have **product**.

And you have **service**.

Their products are the **BEST** . . . the service, is totally a **WOW** experience!

As a customer of Beverly for years, I am **STILL** blown away every time I place an order.

As a matter of fact, every time I either place an order or receive my order in the mail, if there is someone in the room with me, I will immediately brag about what just happened.

I am not an individual who is easily impressed, but I would personally put Beverly International up there with Zappos and Amazon. If you were to speak with the owners, Roger or Sandy Riedinger for any more than a minute, you would know why their customer service is what it is. It is not a service with them, it is a culture. That is a very important distinction. They don't do it as a necessary component to business success; they do it because they genuinely *CARE* about the client. By the way, they call people clients, not customers.

They operate on a deeper level.

"O.K., Jim, that's great, they sound like super people. How and why does that apply to me and my business?"

It applies because their treatment of "clients" has created an *army* of raving fans! The people who use Beverly International products talk about it....*A LOT!* I found this to be fascinating as it is ultra-rare to see this level of excitement from clients or customers in any field. More often than not, the experience is so-so with the occasional pleasant surprise of very good service.

Dealing with Beverly International is far beyond that and their results prove it. With the exception of a few locations, Beverly products are not sold in stores. They are mail order, yet their business continues to thrive.

They also do not spend tens of thousands advertising their products which, in the ultra-competitive supplement industry, is beyond impressive. Most companies crumble under the pressure of going up against competitors with million dollar-advertising budgets.

How do they pull it off?

Their "fans," their incredibly satisfied clients take care of that for them. Word of mouth advertising has always been the best advertising you can get and the Beverly army is out in full force.

This is what you need for your business, an army. It does not matter in any way shape of form what your business is. Even if you are a larger company with a big advertising budget, you must create and keep happy customers.

## Good vs. Bad Customer Service

I'm sure you'll agree that Good Customer service goes a LONG way in helping you and your business. Let's flip the coin and see how BAD customer service can affect your bottom line in a *NEGATIVE* way.

Pay attention. This is the biggest mistake most entrepreneurs make.

As a real estate investor, I buy lots of properties. I also use real estate agents to buy these properties. When I buy properties, all I ask the agent to do is get me the listings, get me in the house, and get my offer in.

That's it.

I am a *dream* client.

A number of years back I was working with a particular agent who had been referred to me. We met. He appeared to be a go-getter so I decided to give him a shot.

Within eight months, I had bought twenty-seven properties from this guy.

Remember what I said about my requirements?

I am basically dropping money in this guy's lap. However, every time I had to call him he acted like it was a pain in the ass. Every time I needed an offer to be submitted on the weekend, it was a pain in the ass. Everything I asked him to do he made me feel like it was . . . right, you guessed it.

The straw that broke the camel's back was this. It was Christmas and I was receiving lots of very nice gifts from people who were very appreciative of the business I was sending them.

I also got something from my agent.

It was a Christmas card with **HIS BUSINESS CARDS** inside. He wanted me to pass them out.

Would you like to wager a guess as to what I did next?

I did some quick math. He was making an average of $2,500 in commission on each deal I purchased.

$2,500 x 27 deals is $67,500 he made from me in eight months. Not only did he make me feel like I was imposing on him, he sends me a Christmas card with his business cards inside?

Are you kidding me?

I never contacted him again, which got his attention very quickly.

He called me and asked why I wasn't contacting him. I told him that I had moved on and that if he had to ask WHY, he would never understand anyway.

---

## The Next Pieces of the Puzzle

Do you think I kept quiet about this?

No.

I told everyone.

I was the CEO of a real estate investment training company with thousands of clients. Guess who they ask for guidance on whom to use? Right. *ME!*

Do you think I recommended him? Nope. Not only did I not recommend him, I used him of an example of the type of realtor that they should **NEVER** use.

How much the long-term cost to him would have been is anyone's guess, but I assure you that it was enough money to buy him a new home and some very nice cars.

Remember, I was not asking him for anything other than to make my life a bit easier and don't get in my way or give me grief. In return I would make him lots of money. I also was not expecting a Christmas gift. But I didn't expect the slap in the face in the form of his Christmas card filled with business cards for me to pass out.

And now yet **ANOTHER** piece of the puzzle.

When you are dealing with a customer, the majority of the time, you have no idea who that person is. Take me for instance. I had a weekly real estate investment radio show on the biggest station in town and had lots of listeners. What if I had decided to tell the story I just told you, on the air?

He would be ruined. I didn't, but many people do.

These days everybody and their brother is a blogger. Some good, some bad. However, many of these people really enjoy getting online and letting everyone know about their bad experiences.

Folks . . . that can destroy your business overnight.

I make it a point to treat everyone I deal with equally. I treat them like a friend. I learned a long time ago that you never know who you are talking to. I have done some big real estate deals with people who, at first glance, looked like they could have been homeless. Instead they were very wealthy investors from the Old Country who were not concerned with the way they looked.

They owned half the neighborhood.

You never know, so don't be stupid.

I strongly suggest you request the bonus interview with Roger and Sandy from Beverly International and adopt their philosophy. Get it at www.sendinthewolves.com I absolutely guarantee you that if you follow that philosophy; it will add money to your bottom line in a big way.

Should you choose the path of "I don't give a shit what people think", well then, good luck. The odds are not in your favor and neither is karma. Do the right thing and watch the money roll in.

---

**Jimmy's Law**

Great customer service is *NOT* an option

# Money, Money, Money…

Now what would a book prospering in business be without a chapter on…MONEY? As I mentioned a number of times throughout the book, the reason we are in business is to make MONEY. Some will say this is shallow and I say they are most likely broke.

This book has been brutally honest so no need to stop now. We are here to make money!

So, how do we do that? Well first of all, I am assuming that you are already making money so I want to talk about how to make MORE money with your existing business or service.

The "Irishman" talked extensively about systems for your business and why they are SO important but that is just one small piece of the puzzle. When we are talking about increasing your cash flow, it is not only about making MORE money but it is also about SAVING you money with your enterprise.

We call this, "Phantom Income". The money that stays in your pocket is as good as someone writing you a check. My experience has been that most businesses are leaking cash flow and some are BLEEDING cash flow.

When John and I are hired by someone, one of the first things we do is get a top down view of every area of the business. This is done with the help of an extensive questionnaire, which gives a very good insight into where we can make the most impact in the shortest amount of time.

As I said, a good part of this is about saving you money so PLEASE do not discount that. A client of ours in California will be able to save $120,000 a YEAR due to real estate cost segregation we employed. That is BEFORE we even got to the MAKING more part. Not too shabby.

This is just one of the cost saving measures we use but as you can see, the impact can be big. Remember, money you don't spend is as good as someone writing you a check.

Now for the making money. There are any number of ways to dramatically increase your business revenue but I will start with one of the obvious and we discuss this in our Send In The Wolves documentary.

RAISE YOUR PRICES....

If you did, would that would that create more revenue for you?  Now I know what you're thinking.  "But Jim, no one will pay me more money"

No, maybe SOME won't pay but you would be shocked how many would.  The methods we use to help you successfully raise your prices is our special sauce.

Here is the cliffs notes version.  Think about what you do and your competition.  Now, how are you different? Are you different or are you all pretty comparable?

For instance, let's say you are a high-end cosmetic dentist.  Most who fall into that category charge high but similar prices.  So what would make someone choose you over your competition when your prices are so much higher?

Answer...FAME!  Yes, FAME as in YOU are the local celebrity.

Being the Author of The Consumer's Guide to Cosmetic Dentistry automatically makes you the go to expert for those who want to say that their dentist is 'The guy that wrote the book"  Oh wait, you DO have the book right? No, you don't but can you see why you DO need one?

Fame = BIG MONEY.

Celebrity sells and once you become the celebrity in your field the flood gates open. How about a trailer and documentary to go along with the book?

Check our what John and I did with our trailer and documentary and I think you will get the picture.

Fame allows you to easily increase prices without resistance from customers in short order. The best thing about this strategy is that practically NO ONE does it. I mean 1 out of 500 will do it but the one who does, owns the game.

You do the math yourself. If you doubled your average transaction size how would that look for your bottom-line?

This leads me to another pricing strategy, which most business owners do not do which is bundling.

I see so many owners and entrepreneurs set in stone at one price but if they would just over a higher priced option and a lower priced option they could dramatically increase revenues. You can do this by bundling products and services together and offering them as opposed to offering them individually.

How about premium pricing?

Do you offer that?

There is always someone that will want the BEST you have to offer so why not create that for them. When I was doing real estate investment seminars I offered packages of $1,500, $6,800 and $20,000.

Guess what?

There was always some that took the 20K package. How much money would be left on the table if I didn't have that to offer? The same goes for the $1,500 price point. What if someone didn't have 20K or $6,800? What if they wanted the service but only had $2,000?

Without that offer you would have walked from 2K.

Are you getting my point?

You can play with your own numbers but what I am trying to tell you is the options you have for pricing are FAR more than you realize.

One more note on PREMIUM pricing. Our recommendation is to ALWAYS be at the top or far over the price points in you field.

NEVER, EVER, try to be the "low cost leader" because you thing that is the only way to get business. You will

NEVER win that game and it is far too stressful and financially stupid to play it. I will say again that with the right systems and positioning in place, price will not be an issue for you.

To get our help in implementing these systems in your business visit:

www.sendinthewolves.com

# Final Word of Warning...

I don't want to burst anyone's bubble, but it's a dirty world out there. You would think that after all these years I would have long since stopped being surprised by what I see happening in the business world.

But I am not.

Not all things are as they may seem and not all people you deal with are well intentioned. On the contrary, many things you see, especially with the internet, are nothing more than smoke and mirrors.

Those so-called *experts* and *gurus* are nothing more than second rate con men hiding behind a website and slick marketing.

To be fair, I am not just talking about making money, self-improvement, business gurus etc. I am talking about every level of business and the government as well.

Let's start with the internet.

As I said in an earlier chapter, the internet can be a blessing and or a curse.

The curse comes in when it becomes the be all and end all for "definitive" information on a given subject. People see something online and they believe it as gospel truth.

One of the world's biggest online *consumer protection* websites where people can go to find out if someone is *reputable* is nothing more than an extortion website.

The Better Business Bureau (BBB) is another *trust worthy* organization people hang their hat on. DO you know you can "buy" a good rating? Shocked? Most people think that the BBB is an organization that provides a public service to protect the public.

Nope.

The BBB is a FOR PROFIT business. Rumor has it that HAMAS, yes the terrorist group, has an A + rating with the BBB.

No joke.

How many times have we seen public figures revered for what they *supposedly* have accomplished, only to find out it was all lies?

The great P.T. Barnum once said, "Never underestimate the ignorance of the general public." He was dead on.

However, let me take it a step further.

I call it **WILLFUL** ignorance.

The gut instinct that we all have that is a warning signal for us is all too often ignored. The bad guys know how to make that happen.

In the seminar world, they employ loud music and fast talking speakers **TELLING** you that you are going to be a big success as long as and only if you work with them. They employ tactics designed to control you and how you think thus making you an easy mark for what they have in store for you.

They call it sales, I call it bullshit.

I'm not saying that every consultant, guru, politician out there is bad or out to harm you. What I am saying is that *most* fall far short of being able to help you. Their combination of skill and ethics is in short supply.

If someone has got the goods, oftentimes they are secretly waiting to prey on the unsuspecting sheep. If someone means well and really wants to provide you with a good product or service, they, too, fall far short on being able to deliver.

In the real estate investment world of which I have been a part of for twenty-seven years now, it is almost laughable in how many new *gurus* and *experts* are out there. Most of them, and I mean **MOST** of them are not even real estate investors nor have they done more than a handful of deals.

Slick marketing and big advertising budgets make up for the shortfall in skill. Can you say, President of the United States? Yup. Here are just a few of the industries I have personally witnessed intentional fraud and corruption:

- Investment Real Estate
- Health Care
- Seminar Industry
- Government
- *Any* of the so-called expert industries
- Sports world
- Consulting Businesses
- Local and National Law enforcement
- Construction Industry
- Marketing

I could go on, by why bother. I think you get the point. It's kind of like a sharp stick in the eye right?

So is it all bad? No, it's not. There are lots of very valuable people in every industry who can not only help you but also do it the right way. The trick is to find them.

Here are a few tips on how to do that:

1.  Believe almost **NOTHING** you read online. In case you did not know, most is either planted and/or created in order to intentionally mislead or fulfill an agenda.

2.  Believe almost **NOTHING** you see in the media, unless it can be substantiated.

3.  Do not be overly persuaded by any type of "Voted Best" types of labels. They can be and *are* purchased.

4.  Put a lot of stock in what is being said about said person and or company by **LEGITMATE** industry leaders. They will not risk their rep to say something good about someone who is not.

5.  Find out what the majority of customers say. Don't look for 100% approval because it doesn't exist. Every now and then a customer gets a bug

up their ass and decides to take revenge on the Internet.

6. ***TRUST YOUR GUT***. This is a very big one that people ignore.

All I am saying is this, be careful out there.

If it seems I have a chip on my shoulder, I do. I don't like fakes, frauds and phonies. Especially when they look for and prey on hard-working folks who are just trying to make their life a little better.

So the million-dollar question is:

### *When is a "bad guy" the good guy?*

Answer . . . when you call the Wolf and the Irishman

For those looking to make life better, make more money, and have more fun and live a life that matters . . . We're on your side. And sometimes, being a good guy just doesn't cut it. Sometimes you need something else. Sometimes you need an equalizer.

***We're the Wolves . . . And we're good people to know . . .***

## Special Message to Anyone Contemplating Starting a Business

Good for you ... smart move. Maybe.

Although much of the content in this book may frighten away fledgling business owners, the flip side of the coin is the financial windfall that can come with being your own boss.

We are not only in the greatest time in history to jump into entrepreneurship, but many people are actually doing it. Tens of thousands of baby boomers, dissatisfied with just existing, are deciding to dive into their own ventures.
As I said, that is great.

However . . . you will most likely get just one shot. Do *not* go blindly into the arena. Smart money surrounds themselves with smart people. For those who do not, that vast majority will fail. Over 50% of new business owners fail in the first few years and over 80% after five years.

How would you like to stack the deck in your favor? I suggest we have a little chat to not only be sure you know what you are getting into, but how you can also have US as the guys who have your back. That, my friends, is money *very* well spent.

# Now What?

Whether you know it or not, if you have read this book closely, you have received a million dollar education. How do we know that? Because well the lessons you learned from Jim alone cost him that much and more.

You get to benefit from his hindsight.

Remember the sayings: "success leaves clues" and "all secrets are visible".

The question that remains is what will you do with the information?

If you're unsure about what to do next or you need guidance, you need systems in your business and you need to actually implement more in your business then the invitation you're about to receive is going to change your business and your life forever.

I have some questions to ask you…

- Are you running a successful business but feel there's room for MORE?
- Are you an ambitious, forward thinking business owner who appreciates and understands the power of having the right people around you?
- Does the idea of having proven to work marketing SYSTEMS in your business that are designed to attract, convert and retail your ideal clients get you excited?
- Do you feel like you have the capacity to be generating more leads, sales, referrals and/or you should be increasing how much each customer/client is worth to you?
- Do you do business from a value first, profit second standpoint where you believe that in order to generate profit you should be adding value to the marketplace?
- Do you take action on your ideas and realize that failure is part of success as long as you learn from it and keep moving forward?
- Do you want to double your income and free time?

If you answered yes to at least five of those questions...it's time to call:

## *The Wolves*

One of the biggest problems many business owners / entrepreneurs face is that they spend far too much time in their own heads and can't see the forest for the trees.

We cannot only see the forest; we can tear it down and rebuild it to suit you.

If you're thinking, "Oh boy, here comes the sales pitch," you would be partially correct.

Yes, we have a unique program called "The Wolf Audit", but we only accept people on a very limited basis . . . we only accept the **RIGHT** businesses and entrepreneurs.

We are fortunate to be able to pick and choose the business owners we work with.

We do not **NEED** to do anything business wise that we do not want to do.

On the other hand, we do **VERY** much enjoy working with the right individuals and businesses in getting them on track, out of trouble, and or doubling their income, freedom and security.

We will tell you freely hiring us privately is not cheap, but we are known as the **WOLVES** for a reason.

We get results…

Period.

If you're interested in being part of an exclusive small, tight knit group of like minded, successful business owners who work together to achieve unparallel profits, professional and personal success then we invite you to apply for one of our coveted Wolf Pack.

The majority of businesses who apply are not accepted but this is a GOOD thing.

We only want to work with the best and you should too.

Our Wolf Audit is the ideal first step as you'll benefit from our two minds working on your business in a way you've never imagined.

No guesswork. No fumbling around in the dark trying to get things done.

Best of all there's no upfront charge for the Wolf Audit. Obviously if we continue working together afterwards there is, but your Wolf Audit is 100% free.

To apply for your Wolf Audit visit www.sendinthewolves.com

# ABOUT JIM TONER

Jim Toner has enjoyed a long career as a real estate investor, radio show host, speaker, and consultant.

He has spoken throughout the country on the value of intelligent real estate investing and has appeared with the likes of Frank McKinney, Bill Bartmann, Sharon Lechter, The Napoleon Hill Foundation, and many more.

Jim's expertise in making real estate investment "user friendly" for the general public has put his services in very big demand. People routinely pay $2,000 to $15,000 and travel from all over the country to attend his real estate investment programs.

Jim, an accomplished entrepreneur who has been in the trenches of the real estate investment world for over twenty-five years, has taught thousands the path towards financial freedom by using his custom *12 Little Houses Plan*.

He is an active philanthropist having been nationally recognized for his work with veterans and the homeless. He is an active member of Frank and Nilsa McKinney's Caring House Project Foundation as well on the Advisory Board Chair of a Pittsburgh, Pennsylvania Salvation Army branch.

He currently works with a limited Private Client Group as well as coaching groups, both of which have waiting lists. He occasionally accepts new private coaching clients on investment real estate and entrepreneurial / business issues.

# ABOUT JOHN MULRY

John Mulry is an award winning and trusted marketing advisor, speaker, and top selling author with a unique, deep knowledge that spans both online and offline direct response marketing. He helps business owners get more customers, referrals and profits through his consulting, his done for you marketing funnels, campaigns, his training courses, books, and his private mastermind groups in conjunction with Jim Toner.

John has sought out and studied under some of the most world-renowned experts in business, direct response marketing and coaching.

Experts including marketing legends Jay Abraham and Dan Kennedy, GKIC, lifestyle and business experts Tony Robbins, Dax Moy, and Emmy award winning movie director/branding agent Nick Nanton.

He lives and breeds by his creeds "invest, consume and act" and having an "expect success attitude". John was handpicked by Dan Kennedy and is Ireland's only GKIC Certified Business Advisor.

In February 2013, John launched first book Your Elephant's Under Threat which received worldwide acclaim from some of the top business and marketing experts worldwide including: top selling author Brian Tracy, world renowned sales trainer Tom Hopkins, Infusionsoft founder Clate Mask, celebrity branding expert Nick Nanton as well as his own mentor and founder of GKIC, Dan Kennedy.

In April 2015, John launched his second book The Truth! – which hit the top sellers three days in a row and received acclaim from customers and clients the world over. He has also launched numerous training programs, courses both online and offline.

In September 2016, John launched his 3rd book Direct Response which again was greatly received and he continues to wow businesses owners with the breadth of knowledge and strategies he possesses to help you attract, convert and retain your most ideal clients.

# Recommended Reading
### (Special note from Jim)

Many people have asked, "Jim, how did you do all this?" For me it all started when I picked up Napoleon Hill's book, *Think and Grow Rich.* Reading that book changed my world.

Charlie "TREMENDOUS" Jones said, "You will be the same person five years from now as you are today except for the books you read and the people you meet."

I made a decision to be a different person. My recommended reading list is constantly expanding.

Here are a few books that I would recommend be a part of anyone's library.

Albom, Mitch – *Tuesdays with Morrie: An Old Man, a Young Man and Life's Greatest Lessons, The Five People You Meet in Heaven*

Bartmann, Bill – *Billionaire Secrets to Success, Bouncing Back*

Brady, Shelly – *Ten Things I Learned from Bill Porter*

Brown, Les – *It's Not Over Until You Win*

Camp, Jim – *Start with NO*

Canfield, Jack – *Dare to Win*

Clason, George S. – *The Richest Man in Babylon*

Collins, Jim – *Good to Great*

Cousins, Norman – *Anatomy of an Illness*

Dennis, Felix – *How to Get Rich*

Eker, T. Harv – *Secrets of the Millionaire Mind*

Harnish, Verne – *Mastering the Rockefeller Habits*

Gitomer, Jeffrey – *The Sales Bible*

Haggai, John E. – *Paul J. Meyer and the Art of Giving*

Hill, Napoleon – *Think and Grow Rich, Positive Action Plan*

Hoffer, Eric – *The True Believer*

Jones, Charlie – *Life is Tremendous*

Keith, Kent M. – *Anyway: The Paradoxical Commandments*

Kennedy, Dan – *No B.S. Marketing to the Affluent, No B.S. Ruthless Management of People and Profits, No B.S. Direct Marketing, No B.S. Wealth Attraction for Entrepreneurs, No B.S. Sales Success, No B.S. Time Management for Entrepreneurs*

Kroc, Ray – *Grinding It Out: The Making of McDonalds*

Kushner, Harold S. – *Living a Life that Matters*

Landrum, Gene N. – *Profiles of Power and Success, The Superman Syndrome*

Lechter, Sharon – *Three Feet from Gold: Turn Your Obstacles into Opportunities*

Mandino, Og – *The Greatest Salesman in the World, A Better Way to Live, The Greatest Miracle in the World, The Greatest Secret in the World, Og Mandino's University of Success*

McKinney, Frank – *Burst This!, The Tap, Dead Fred, Flying Lunchboxes, The Good Luck Circle, and Make It Big*

Mulry, John – *Your Elephant's Under Threat, The Truth!, Direct Response*

Olson, Jeff – *The Slight Edge*

Peters, Thomas J. – *In Search of Excellence*

Peters, Tom – *Re-Imagine!*

Proctor, Bob – *It's Not About the Money*

Robert, Cavett – *Success with People*

Rohn, Jim – *The Seasons of Life*

Stovall, Jim – *The Ultimate Gift*

Wilde, Stuart – *The Trick to Money is Having Some*

Wooden, John – *The Essential Wooden*

# NOTES

# NOTES

www.ingramcontent.com/pod-product-compliance
Lightning Source LLC
Chambersburg PA
CBHW020153200326
41521CB00006B/351